Foundations of Software Design

J. F. Leathrum
Department of Electrical and
Computer Engineering
Clemson University

 RESTON PUBLISHING COMPANY, INC.
A *Prentice-Hall Company*
Reston, Virginia

Library of Congress Cataloging in Publication Data

Leathrum, J. F.
    Foundations of software design.

    1. Electronic digital computers—Programming.
I. Title.
QA76.6.L364 1982   001.64'25   82–20540
ISBN 0–8359–2094–1

Editorial/production supervision and
interior design by Camelia Townsend

10 9 8 7 6 5 4 3 2 1

PRINTED IN THE UNITED STATES OF AMERICA

This book is dedicated to my family whose consideration has been essential to the fulfillment of the task. To my wife Barbara's indomitable spirit, to Jim's gritty courage, to Tom's penetrating questions, and to Roger's never say can't persistence. These have all been an invaluable inspiration.

Contents

Appendices

Preface

This book is intended to serve as a textbook for upper-level undergraduates and beginning graduate students in computer science, management science, and engineering. It brings together material that has appeared as collections of papers in several volumes. The purpose here is to achieve a single coordinated volume suitable for classroom use. The subject of software design is clearly deserving of some academic attention since it has already profoundly changed our way of thinking about computing and programming.

"Software design" is a reasonably descriptive term for a subject sometimes known as software engineering, software reliability, or simply, programming. This text deals primarily with the human and social aspects of programming, but the subject is clearly a technical one in its concern for the tools of software construction, design methodologies, and analysis of observations about software.

Although the subject of programming methodology is included in this book, there is no intent that only this text be used to cover the treatment of programming methodology. If this book is to be used in a full year course that includes in-depth treatment of programming methodology, some supplementary material would be required.

It is the nature of software design that the level of mathematical vigor varies from topic to topic. It helps to observe that most other design disciplines share this feature. After all, an engineer cannot justify avoiding design issues simply because the mathematical foundations are undeveloped or because the quantitative basis of a technique is based on purely empirical knowledge. In the case of software design, the lack of vigor is most apparent in the discussion of requirements statements (Chapter 3). The imminent development of vigor is evident in the testing technology (Chapter 7), and the well-developed mathematical foundations are apparent in programming methodology (Chapter 5).

The material included in this text has been taught in one-semester upper-level undergraduate courses and one-semester graduate courses. In both cases, the courses include requirements for a software design project and report. The faster-paced graduate course is usually supplemented with additional text material in programming methodology. It is suggested that a graduate course based on this text be followed by a course in programming methodology for multiprocessor systems (e.g., Problem 2, page 122).

The author is indebted to Tulane University, the University of Delaware, and Clemson University for their support of the development of this text. The patience and understanding of the students of these universities who have used preliminary versions of the text are acknowledged with gratitude. Particular thanks goes to Mrs. C. Calcutt for assisting with the typing of the final manuscript, and to R. Fulbright, M. Gearhart, and W. Godfrey for their assistance in the preparation of examples and exercises.

J. F. Leathrum

Software Engineering in Scientific and Historical Perspective

1.1   The Software Experience

1.1 THE SOFTWARE EXPERIENCE

The current state of software technology is a product of a variety of technical and economic pressures both historic and contemporary. Since the advent of the digital computer, there has been a nearly complete inversion of economic incentive in the design and implementation of programs (software). In the earliest days, computer memory seemed to be the most constraining resource to the programmer. Both programmer and machine time were important considerations, but until the demand for programmers and machines increased, these were not constraining resources. (A convenient way to relive the earliest software experience is to develop a program for one of the extant programmable pocket calculators.) To the programmer, the primary objective in such situations is to achieve so-called "tight" code. The code itself could not be allowed to occupy very much space. Since the program never became very large, the understanding of the underlying program structure was not very difficult.

The memory constraints upon programs were released quite dramatically with the advent of core memories, but execution time remained a serious constraint until processor technology advanced. The "time-efficiency" of a program was an issue that also forced the generation of tight code. Under this pressure, concerns for program structure were prostituted in order to save a few machine cycles. Programming was viewed as a process of synthesizing very small pieces of code into a whole program. The early use of the word *compiler* suggests this view.

EXERCISE 1–1

Develop a computer program for approximating $\cos(\theta)$ for $\theta = 45° + i'$; $i = 0, 1, 2, \ldots 59$ using the Taylor Series approximation. Assume the total memory is restricted to 100 cells. Each instruction and each number require one cell of memory. Employ a typical computer instruction set, but do not assume the existence of floating point instructions. (*Note*: This was the author's first programming assignment in a first-semester calculus class in 1955. The computer was the EDVAC at Aberdeen Proving Ground, Md.)

Hindsight suggests that programmers should have avoided the early pitfalls of software, particularly since many programmers were engineers. It is not unusual, however, for a technology to evolve through such an experience. It can even be argued from experiences in other

2

technologies such as bridge building that this early stage in the evolution of programming technology was inevitable. The renaissance was virtually assured by the experience of the OS-360 operating system for the IBM-360 computer. Thousands of man-years were committed to the development of that software. The assessment of the performance of the system is debatable, but it is generally agreed that it never performed as planned. There is little question that the OS-360 operating system was difficult and costly to maintain. The OS-360 experience was so negative that it has become a point of reference in most discussions of software phenomenology (see Chapter 2).

Almost concurrent with the development of the OS-360 software, a small group led by E. W. Dijkstra in the Netherlands was developing the THE (Technische Hogeschool of Eindhoven) operating system. The product of the THE effort was primarily methodological (see Table 1–1). It led to Dijkstra's meteoric emergence as the answer to the OS-360 debacle. He single-handedly reoriented the concerns in programming and software design.

In retrospect, the decade spanning the period of 1968 to 1978 must be regarded as unique in the development of software engineering. Prior to this period, interest was primarily focused on the creation of the widest variety of tools, languages, and methodologies. The conventional wisdom of the time argued that more and bigger were better. The phenomenon is best exemplified by the creation of PL/I as a programming language and by the experimentation with extensible languages. Although the latter had very little impact on software design methodology, it was nonetheless guided by the premises that the methodology could be improved by adding more and more tools. To the practicing programmer and programming organizations, the practice of analysis in minutiae was the byword of the trade. There was a presumption that any problem could be solved by the use of ever more specialized tools applied to increasingly microscopic views of software. (Even programmer aptitude tests reflected this concern for microanalysis.)

The period from 1968 to 1978 was a period of deep doubts and questioning about the priority of concerns in software engineering. The small and simple captured the attention of both the researchers and the practitioners. The UNIX* operating system and the programming language "C" are well-known products of this period. The principle was well stated by the UNIX designers:

> To many, the UNIX systems embody Schumacher's dictum, "Small is beautiful...." [From MPT78, p. 1890]

---

* UNIX is a trademark of the Bell Laboratories.

TABLE 1-1

MILESTONES IN SOFTWARE TECHNOLOGY

Software	Designer	Period of Major Design and Implementation Activity	Technological Significance
Fortran Compiler	IBM	1954–1958	First high-level language tools.
B-5500 Algol	Burroughs Corp.	1961–1964	Machine designed for software compatibility; Algol used as a "systems programming language."
THE	Dijkstra	1963–1965	Precursor to structured programming.
OS-360	IBM	1963–1967	First major *design* failure.
Pl/I Compiler	IBM	1963–1968	Creation of a large array of software design tools in a high-level language.
MULTICS	M.I.T.	1965–1969	Integrated hardware–software systems design. Joint project with academic and industrial participation.
Safeguard	U.S. Dept. of Defense	1972–	Intensified the awareness in the defense community of the high cost of software.
Ada	U.S. Dept. of Defense	1980–	A new start in the creation of software design tools.

The methodologies that developed during this period also employed a small number of building blocks. Program construction was to be understood by a process of abstraction—abstraction away from the irrelevant features of building blocks. Software systems were judged by their simplicity and design integrity and not by the extent of use of specialized tools and language features.

In the context of these inexorable crosscurrents, it is worthwhile to reconsider Dijkstra's original premise as paraphrased here:

1. Construction of correct programs requires that the programs be intellectually manageable.
2. The key to intellectual manageability is the structure of the program itself.
3. Disciplined use of a few program building blocks facilitates correctness arguments.

Dijkstra has contributed in many ways to the development of programming methodology, but two works stand out as having particularly significant impact. First, he opened the Go To controversy by writing "Go To Statement Considered Harmful" (Di68). Here his message was essentially as just stated, but the title and focus of that paper led to a diversion of the discourse as to whether Go To's should be a part of programming languages. Second, his contribution to *Structured Programming* (DDH72) provided a thorough exposition of his thinking about program structures. The force of the person and the eloquence of the message cannot be overstated in the assessment of the events that followed, but it is also fair to observe that the time for change was at hand. The economic and technical pressures for a new methodology were so great that change was inevitable.

The period from 1968 through 1978 was a period of reaction to the excesses and mistakes that led up to Dijkstra's principles of structured programming. The theoretical foundations of programming were consolidated, and a number of useful design techniques emerged. The new programming has now matured to the point that we can think in terms of teaching it at all levels.

The period subsequent to 1978 has been characterized by some reaction to the unfulfilled expectations of the new methodology. Pitfalls within the theoretical foundations have been identified, and competing methodologies have been found to complement each other (e.g., verification and testing methodology).

Another strange phenomenon has occurred since 1978, in that there has been some regression to the pre-1968 era of software engineering. Some of the impetus for this regression has come from the impact of highly integrated computer hardware designs for which little software methodology has been developed. Ironically, the most visible attempt to solve the software problem, the Ada programming language (Chapter 4, Section 4.5, and Appendix A-2), represents in itself a regression. Although Ada, as a software design tool, addresses problems not heretofore solved, the language itself suffers from unwieldy size and is burdened by too many building blocks.

EXERCISE 1-2

Using a high-level language such as Algol or Pl/I, develop a program for the Bubble Sort algorithm without the use of Go To. To what extent were new variables introduced to overcome the absence of Go To?

REFERENCES

(DDH72)   Dahl, O. J., E. W. Dijkstra, and C. A. R. Hoare, *Structured Programming*. New York: Academic Press, Inc., 1972.

(Di68)   Dijkstra, E. W., "Go To Statement Considered Harmful," *Communications of the ACM,* vol. 11 (1968).

(MPT78)   McIlroy, M. D., E. N. Pinson, and B. A. Tague, "Unix Time-Sharing System: Foreword," *The Bell System Technical Journal,* 57 (1978), 1899–1904.

Software
Phenomenology

Coincident with the emerging concerns about program structure, questions have been raised about fundamental principles that govern the design and maintenance of software. Equally intriguing is the question of whether these principles can be verified experimentally. The situation is the classical one that has arisen several times in physics wherein a general theory is proposed and there follows a phase of experimentation to either prove or disprove the theory. This approach to understanding software in terms of the phenomenology is a fairly recent development from which some valuable insights have already emerged.

2.1 THE SOFTWARE LIFE CYCLE

It is useful to analyze the software phenomenon in terms of a typical software life cycle. From such a viewpoint the observable quantities can be identified, and the modeling can be focused on well-circumscribed activities. The life cycle is best viewed as a succession of steps:

1. Requirements statement
2. Software design
3. Coding
4. Testing
5. Maintenance

Refinements of this breakdown will be considered in subsequent chapters. Thus, for the purpose of this section, it suffices to think of the various phases in very simple terms: (1) a requirements statement involves stating the purpose of the software: what is to be done, not how it is to be done; (2) software design is primarily a process of modularization of the software into pieces that can be implemented on a computer; (3) coding is the process of translating a design into a programming language; (4) testing involves both functional testing of each module as well as integration tests of the entire software package; and (5) maintenance arises in the process of perfecting the implementation and in responding to changes in the requirements for the software.

In observing software as it passes through such a life cycle, some metrics must be adopted in order to attain quantitative insights. The obvious life cycle metrics in this case are money, error rates, and time. It is possible through direct observation to conclude that maintenance is by far the most costly phase of the life cycle. This phase typically accounts for 70 percent of the total cost (see Figure 2–1).

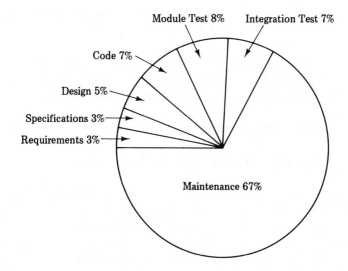

Figure 2-1. True Effort in Many Large-Scale Software Systems. (From Ze78, p. 199; used with permission.)

This simple observation can be quite misleading, however, unless it is noted that maintenance involves the elimination of errors incurred in the other phases as well as a response to changing requirements. The technical problem becomes one of developing the tools to correct errors (testing and maintenance) plus formulating techniques to avoid the errors in the first place (design and implementation). The experimental evidence points to design as being the largest contributor to software errors and thus to the overall cost (BL79). Here design is understood to include both the requirements statement and software design phases of the life cycle.

The duration of the software life cycle is somewhat variable and susceptible to subtle changes in methodology. It is not unusual to have software projects last six to ten years when all of the releases and updates are included up to a point of apparent obsolescence. During such a lifetime, the cycle is likely to be repeated several times. New requirements or new designs may be proposed for part or all of the software, and each of these modifications would pass through the entire cycle. Thus, the life cycle is best viewed as a recursion of similar cycles within the phase identified as "maintenance." The total duration is primarily dependent on the total number of recurrences permitted before a new model is designed.

EXERCISE 2-1

Compare this discussion of the software life cycle with similar cycles in other areas of human activity (e.g., writing a book, taking a vacation, building a boat, etc.). What are the unique features of the software life cycle?

2.2 REPLACEMENT OF SOFTWARE

An interesting comparison of the replacement of software with new models versus the replacement policies in other areas is provided by Belady and Lehman (BL79). They note some irrational resistance to replacing software when compared to automobiles or even when compared to biological evolution. The recognition of this phenomenon has stimulated much of the interest in formulating models of the software life cycle.

The irrational and somewhat uncanny attachment that forms between the creator of software and the software itself is manifested in many forms. Most prominently we see the phenomenon in compilers and in operating systems that are employed by software implementors. The programming languages and the systems interfaces take on a mother tongue quality. We even begin to think in terms of the language or interface that has been created. A good example of this is the development and refinement of Lisp. Lisp is a programming language that was developed in the period from 1958 to 1962 and was originally implemented on the IBM 704...7094 machine architecture. The developers of the language adopted the acronyms "CAR" and "CDR" to mean "contents of A register" and "contents of D register," respectively. The machines have long since become obsolete, but the use of CAR and CDR lives on in the lexicon of Lisp.

Although this longevity of languages and operating systems is more complex than a simple attachment of the creator to the object created, it is symptomatic of the phenomenon. It is seen more clearly as software progresses from a program to a programming systems product (see Section 2.6).

At least a part of the reluctance to replace software is a natural consequence of the ever-recurring life cycle during maintenance. The tendency to create ever more complex structures during maintenance, together with the turnover of personnel involved, is likely to create a fear of major overhaul. Unfortunately there are numerous examples of software products that continue to evolve and become so complex that correctness and usefulness begin to deteriorate. Although the phenomenon is readily recognized after the fact, it remains very difficult to detect in time to divert the maintenance effort into the creation of a new product.

The keys to economical and rational replacement policies seem to lie in two areas:

1. The development of experimentally verifiable models of the software life cycle (BL79), and

2. The use of design methodologies that preclude the degradation during maintenance (see Chapter 4).

2.3 PRODUCTIVITY AND CREATIVITY

As an aside, it should be noted that observations of human productivity and creativity in software production remain illusive and unreliable. The coding activity has been measured in terms of lines per day, but here the productivity is highly sensitive to the language and methodology being employed. For a thorough discussion of this point, see *The Mythical Man-Month* (Br75). Productivity measures are not very meaningful in the design phases since this is a highly creative activity. The combination of the creative element and variety of language tools tends to suggest that the software industry is a cottage industry and may remain so for some time.

It is with respect to productivity that the software phenomenon faces a yet to be resolved dilemma. Given what is apparently a big job, we either commit resources to "getting on with it" or we commit resources to "making it small." The situation is very much like the decision to write a novel or to write a poem. In both software and the literary analog we are dealing with a highly creative activity. The approach that we take to the production aspects of the task is largely subject to individual and managerial bias, and sometimes is even dictated by the tools being employed. (Perhaps there would have been Twenty Commandments had the tablets been more pliable.) It is not at all uncommon to hear a programmer observe that the simplest of concepts may be very difficult to express concisely in some programming language.

2.4 PROGRAM SCALE

The issue of scale has been a central issue in the phenomenology of software since the first awareness of the design problem. Here the concern is what makes a program large as well as how is largeness measured. The

fact that there is a distinct incomparability between small and large programs has been recognized for some time. Linear metrics for size such as
lines of code, number of inputs, etc., have not adequately captured the
nature of the scale differences. Belady and Lehman suggest an appealing
definition of largeness that leads to an entropy-like model of structure:

> A program is large if it reflects within itself a variety of human interests and
> activities. [BL79, p. 108]

The key to this definition is the notion of "variety." As noted by the
authors, the definition almost immediately suggests a capability and
structure for large programs that would be beyond the intellectual grasp
of a single individual.

The recognition of variety as an important element in large-scale
software, in turn, suggests two fundamental laws as proposed by Belady
and Lehman (BL79, pp. 112–114):

1. *Law of Continuing Change:* A software system will undergo continuing change until it is judged cost effective to freeze and recreate
   it.
2. *Law of Increasing Unstructuredness:* A software system will become
   more unstructured with time unless specific work is executed to
   maintain or reduce it.

These "laws" have been formulated in a way quite similar to the laws of
thermodynamics. They suggest a dynamism of software that is somewhat analogous to the motion of gaseous molecules. The notion of
equilibrium appears to be missing in this framework. It is suggested that
equilibrium is never attained due to the fact that the desire to perfect
software and the inevitable change in the requirements maintain the
force for continuing change.

As noted in Section 2.2, the judgment as to when software should
be frozen and recreated remains devoid of adequate economic or technical guidelines. It can only be observed from the past that there is a
tendency amongst software maintainers to patch rather than renew. It
appears that a unique bond forms between a program and its creator that
inhibits rational decisions to buy or create a new program. The price we
pay for our poor judgment is clearly stated in the second law noted
above.

The phenomenological approach to software is still developing
along several lines. The borrowing of principles from the physical
sciences is best exemplified by the work of Halstead (Ha77), wherein he
coined the term *software physics.* Common physical notions of length,

volume, level, etc., are developed, and models are employed to describe the behavior of software. This approach is further elaborated in the next section.

In spite of the apparent insights gained from observing and modeling the behavior of software, nothing as profound or precise as Newton's laws of motion has emerged. It has been suggested that the real software problem is a management one. The management problem is acute because the software development tools are primitive and because, as yet, no satisfactory means of passing knowledge and experience to a new generation of specialists has been developed. This was particularly evident in the Project MAC experience at M.I.T. They found a serious scarcity of persons with experience from a previous project. Mistakes were inevitably repeated because the experience had no medium of transferral (CC77).

2.5 SOFTWARE PHYSICS

A branch of the study of software phenomena has developed through the analysis and experiments conceived by M. H. Halstead (Ha77). He focuses attention on the properties of *representations* of algorithms. The objective is to make quality judgments about representations and to make predictions about the size of representations and the programming effort to create them given a particular repertoire of programming tools.

Halstead builds a theoretical framework on software metrics and shows how the theory can be validated. The theory is based on the following fundamental notions (Ha77):

Length: The total usage of all operators and operands in a representation of a program.

Length Equation: The length of a program may be approximated by

$$\hat{N} = \eta_1 \log_2 \eta_1 + \eta_2 \log_2 \eta_2$$

where η_1 is the total number of distinct operators in a representation and η_2 is the total number of distinct operands in a representation. He finds that the values of length obtained from the Length Equation agree very well with counts obtained according to the definition of length (see Figure 2–2).

In addition to the notion of length, Halstead suggests a derived framework of properties of representations of programs. First, in order to factor out irrelevant differences in languages that appear in the

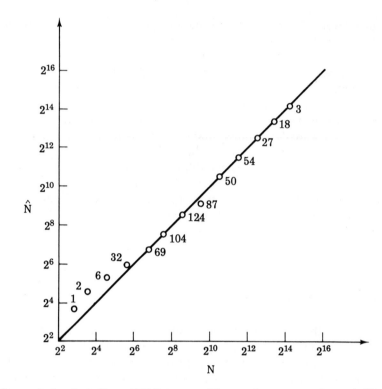

Figure 2-2.   Data From 577 Programs (N vs. $\eta_1 \log_2 \eta_1 + \eta_2 \log_2 \eta_2$). (From Ha77, p. 16; used with permission.)

representation of programs, Halstead suggests the following constraints (Ha77). First, a *volume metric* is defined as shown below:

$$\text{Volume} = \text{length} \times \log_2 (\eta_1 + \eta_2)$$

The volume is bound from below by noting that a program would have at least two operators and no less than one occurrence of each operator and operand. This leads to the *potential volume*, V*:

$$V^* = (2 + \eta_2^*) \log_2 (2 + \eta_2^*)$$

where η_2^* is the number of input/output parameters. The potential volume is clearly language-independent. A less idealized lower bound is obtained by use of the Length Equation. This is called the *boundary volume*, V**:

$$V^{**} = (2 + \eta_2^* \log_2 \eta_2^*) \times \log_2 (2 + \eta_2^*)$$

The *level* of implementation of an algorithm, L, is used to represent the divergence from the potential volume. Thus,

$$V^* = L \times V$$

where $L \leq 1$, and a validated means of approximating this level is given by

$$L = \left(\frac{2}{\eta_1}\right) \cdot \left(\frac{\eta_2}{N_2}\right)$$

where N_2 is the total number of instances of operands (see Table 2-1). The estimated level can be obtained directly from the text of a representation. Thinking of potential volume as a fundamental measure of information in an algorithm, a surrogate is proposed using the estimated level.

TABLE 2-1

THE PROGRAM LEVEL RELATIONSHIP

Algorithm Number	η_2^*	η_1	η_2	N_2	N	L	$\hat{L}$
				Observed Parameters		Level	
CACM 1	8	10	18	56	104	0.066	0.064
CACM 2	3	14	8	37	84	0.031	0.031
CACM 3	12	18	41	220	454	0.020	0.021
CACM 4	5	16	21	61	137	0.028	0.043
CACM 5	4	15	16	60	124	0.025	0.036
CACM 6	4	15	13	42	99	0.033	0.041
CACM 7	3	10	9	29	59	0.046	0.062
CACM 8	5	15	16	60	133	0.030	0.036
CACM 9	10	19	41	162	312	0.023	0.027
CACM 10	3	9	9	25	48	0.058	0.080
CACM 11	3	9	9	29	55	0.051	0.069
CACM 12	3	11	9	31	62	0.043	0.053
CACM 13	3	11	8	30	61	0.045	0.048
CACM 14	7	15	25	91	187	0.029	0.037
GM 15	32	27	100	301	686	0.036	0.025
GM 28	43	49	214	944	1919	0.016	0.009
GM 36	68	47	329	1318	2642	0.019	0.011
GM 40	58	82	433	1944	3985	0.010	0.005
GM 50	32	35	168	584	1248	0.018	0.016
GM 118	6	13	24	57	122	0.038	0.065
Mean						0.033	0.039
Coefficient of correlation						0.90	

From Ha77, p. 29; used with permission.

Thus,

$$I = \hat{L} \times V$$

where I is called the *intelligence content*. It is found to be nearly invariant over representations of an algorithm in a variety of languages.

Halstead notes that this invariance must be qualified to apply to programs that are in some sense "pure." It is quite possible to have wide variations in the intelligence content for an algorithm in a single language through the introduction of extraneous operators and operands (impurities). There is a close correspondence between the removal of impurities and program optimization as performed by compilers. The question of whether "pure" programs are better programs is left open by Halstead (Ha77).

Halstead proceeds to develop models of programming effort, programmer time, and language level in terms of the measures already discussed (Ha77). The programming effort is derived to be

$$E = \frac{V^2}{V^*}$$

or proportional to the square of the volume. The advantage of modularization is evident by noting that if

$$V = \sum_i v_i$$

where v_i is the volume of the ith module, then

$$\sum_i v_i^2 \leq V^2$$

The *programmer's time* may be expressed in terms of both effort, E, and the speed of mental discriminations, S. This S is developed from psychological reasoning due to Stroud and is known as the Stroud number (seconds). It may take on values of 5 to 20. Halstead uses a value of 18 for software (Ha77). It has been argued that the time

$$T = \frac{E}{S}$$

is best used to measure the time to read and understand a program (FL78). Because of the uncertainties in the psychological factors in the time equation, it seems to express little more than the idea that programming time is proportional to effort.

TABLE 2-2

INTELLIGENCE CONTENT I OF ALGORITHM CACM 13
IN VARIOUS LANGUAGES

Language	I
Algol 58	14
Fortran	15
Cobol	16
Basic	15
Snobol	16
APL	16
PL/I	16

From Ha77, p. 36; used with permission.

EXERCISE 2-2

Using the "programmer's time" equation with a Stroud number of 18, estimate the time to do Exercise 1-2 (i.e., Bubble Sort without Go To). How well does the estimate agree with the actual time?

The *language level* is proposed as a means of capturing the differences between languages. Here, Halstead proposes λ as a metric, where

$$\lambda = LV^* = L^2V$$

Using this definition, he has been able to rank languages in a way that is intuitively correct, i.e., English prose as the highest and assembler as the lowest. When the language level is combined with the effort equation,

$$E = \frac{(V^*)^3}{\lambda^2}$$

one finds a dramatic $1/\lambda^2$, showing the effect of language level on effort. Observing from Halstead's data that the level of PL/I is about twice the level of an assembler (Ha77), one could expect a factor of four savings in effort through the use of PL/I.

Errors are always of interest in measuring properties of software. Halstead proposes the *number of delivered errors*, B, and represents it as

$$B = L \times \frac{E}{E_0}$$

TABLE 2–3

MEAN AND VARIANCE OF LANGUAGE LEVEL
FOR SEVEN LANGUAGES

Language	λ	Variance
English	2.16	0.74
PL/I	1.53	0.92
Algol 58	1.21	0.74
Fortran	1.14	0.81
Pilot	0.92	0.43
Assembly	0.88	0.42

From Ha77, p. 68; used with permission.

where $E_0 \approx 3000$ (Ha77). This leads to the means of estimating the number of errors as

$$\hat{B} = \frac{E^{2/3}}{3000}$$

or

$$\hat{B} = \frac{V}{3000}$$

Once again, the estimator has been subjected to experimental validation.

Software physics has been called an "actuarial" approach to software (De78, FL78). It provides gross estimates of properties of collections of software, but it extends to individual cases somewhat unreliably. Thus, one should not think of the "laws" as laws of nature and thus free of restrictions in level of detail and technological change. The theory does, however, provide a framework for observations about software, and quite reliably ranks the occurrences correctly. Since the ranking may be all that is needed (i.e., language level rankings), and may be all that is obtainable due to technical and psychological considerations, the theory may be overparameterized. More definitive and reliable statements may be possible through the use of nonparametric statistics applied to the same data.

Example 2–1   *Analysis of a program for Gaussian elimination.*

The program below is an implementation of a Gaussian elimination algorithm represented in Fortran. The program is reprinted from DLS79, pp. 338–339.

```
C               —Subroutine GAUSS
C                   Subprogram to reduce a system of N equations
C                   in N unknowns, T*X = C, to triangular form
C NDIM          —dimensioned (available) size of all arrays
C N             —array size (actual) for problem to be solved
C T             —import matrix (general) and export matrix (triangular)
C C             —import and export form of right-hand-side vector
C FLAG          —FLAG − 1 if a diagonal element of (triangular) T is 0
C MAX           —largest (in magnitude) subdiagonal element
C INDEX         —row containing the largest subdiagonal element
C RATIO         —ratio of subdiagonal to diagonal element
      SUBROUTINE  GAUSS  (NDIM,N,T,C,FLAG)
      INTEGER NDIM, N, I, J, K, INDEX, FLAG
      REAL T(NDIM,NDIM), C(NDIM), MAX, TEMP, RATIO, ABS
C Create zeros in subdiagonal positions of columns 1 to N − 1.
C Check for zero diagonal elements in the reduction.
      FLAG = 0
      I = 0
      WHILE(I .LE. N − 1) DO
C         Find the maximum subdiagonal element in column I.
      INDEX = 1
      MAX = ABS(T(I,I))
      J = I + 1
      WHILE(J .LE. N) DO
          IF(ABS(T(J,I)) .GT. MAX) THEN DO
              MAX = ABS(T(J,I))
              INDEX = J
          END IF
          J = J + 1
      END WHILE
C         IF INDEX exceeds I, exchange rows INDEX and I.
      IF (INDEX .GT. I) THEN DO
              K = I
              WHILE(K .LE. N) DO
```

```
                    TEMP = T(I,K)
                    T(I,K) = T(INDEX,K)
                    T(INDEX,K) = TEMP
                    K = K + 1
                END WHILE
                TEMP = C(I)
                C(I) = C(INDEX)
                C(INDEX) = TEMP
        END IF
C       If the maximum pivot element is zero, set FLAG = 1 and
C       bypass the row operations at stage I.
        IF(MAX .EQ. 0) THEN DO
                FLAG = 1
                I = I + 1
        ELSE DO
C               For nonzero pivot, create zeros in subdiagonal
C               positions of column I by row operations.
                J = I + 1
                WHILE(J .LE. N) DO
                    K = I + 1
                    RATIO = T(J,I)/T(I,I)
                    WHILE (K .LE. N) DO
                        T(J,K) = T(J,K) - T(I,K)*RATIO
                        K = K + 1
                    END WHILE
                    C(J) = C(J) - C(I)*RATIO
                    J = J + 1
                END WHILE
                I = I + 1
        END IF
    END WHILE
    RETURN
    END
```

(a) OPERATORS (η_1)

The SEQUENTIAL control structure is included. Assignment (=) is counted as an operator. Since this is a subroutine, a CALL and a RETURN are also included. The WHILE..DO, IF..THEN control structures are used. Numerical and logical operators .LE., ABS, .GT., .EQ., +, −, /, *, complete the operators:

OPERATORS

SEQ, WHILE.. DO, IF.. THEN,
ABS, .LE., .GT., .EQ., +, $\eta_1 = 14$
−, /, *, =, CALL, RETURN

(b) OPERANDS (η_2)

The subroutine declarations and the integer/real declarations enumerate the operands:

OPERANDS

NDIM, N, FLAG,
I, J, K, INDEX, T(array),
C(array), MAX, TEMP,
RATIO $\eta_2 = 12$

(*Note:* ABS has been counted as an operator.)

(c) I/O PARAMETERS

Looking at the subroutine definition statement, all operands within the parentheses are I/O parameters to the subroutine:

NDIM, N, T, C, FLAG $\eta_2^* = 5$

(d) TOTAL NUMBER OF OCCURRENCES

Counting each occurrence of the above operands (not including the INTEGER, REAL, or subroutine definition statements), we have:

$$N_2 = 69$$

(e) IN SUMMARY

$$\eta_1 = 14 \qquad N_2 = 69 \qquad S = 18$$
$$\eta_2 = 12 \qquad \eta_2^* = 5$$

(f) COMPUTING THE ESTIMATES

$$\hat{N} = \eta_1 \log_2 \eta_1 + \eta_2 \log_2 \eta_2$$
$$= 14 \log_2 14 + 12 \log_2 12$$
$$= 96$$

$$V = \hat{N} \log_2 (\eta_1 + \eta_2)$$
$$= 96 \log_2 26$$
$$= 451$$

$$V^* = (2 + \eta_2^*) \log_2 (2 + \eta_2^*)$$
$$= (2 + 5) \log_2 (2 + 5)$$
$$= 20$$

$$V^{**} = (2 + \eta_2^* \log_2 \eta_2^*) [\log_2 (2 + \eta_2^*)]$$
$$= (7 \log_2 5)(\log_2 7)$$
$$= 46$$

$$L = \frac{V^*}{V} = \frac{20}{451} \qquad \hat{L} = \left(\frac{2}{\eta_1}\right)\left(\frac{\eta_2}{N_2}\right)$$
$$= .044 \qquad\qquad\quad = \left(\frac{2}{14}\right)\left(\frac{12}{69}\right)$$
$$\hat{L} = .025$$

$$I = \hat{L}V$$
$$= (0.25)(451)$$
$$= 11.20$$

$$\lambda = LV^* = (.044)(20)$$
$$= .88$$

$$E = \frac{V^2}{V^*} = \frac{(451)^2}{20}$$

$$= 10{,}170$$

$$T = \frac{E}{S} = \frac{10{,}170}{18}$$

$$= 565$$

$$B = L(E/E_0) \qquad \text{where } E_0 = 3000$$

$$= .044\,\frac{10170}{3000}$$

$$= 0.15$$

$$\hat{B} = \frac{E^{2/3}}{E_0} = \frac{(10170)^{2/3}}{3000}$$

$$= 0.16$$

Example 2-2 *Analysis of a search program written in an assembly language.*

The language chosen here is the Intel 8080/8085 assembly language. The program text is as follows:

```
Prog: IN         OOH          ; word to match
      MVI        E,N          ; length of buffer
      LXI        H, Buffer    ; address of buffer
Here: CMP        M            ; compare of first word
      JZ         OUT          ; match end program
      DCR        E            ; decrement counter
      JZ         OUT          ; exit on zero count
      INX        H            ; move buffer pointer
      JMP        Here         ; loop back no match
Out:  END        Prog         ; end of program
                              ; (E > 0) = > found
```

The first step in any calculation is to count the number of distinct operands and operators, as follows:

Operands	Total Usage
(1) Word to be matched	2
(2) Length of buffer	2
(3) Address of buffer	3
(4) Program label "Here"	3
(5) Program label "Out"	1
(6) Result of compare	2

Operators	Total Usage
IN	1
MVI	1
LXI	1
CMP	1
JZ	2
DCR	1
INX	1
JMP	1
SEQuential	1

The length is a count of the total usage of all operators and operands. In this representation, N = 22. Halstead states that $N \approx \hat{N}$ (Ha77), where

$$\hat{N} = \eta_1 \log_2 \eta_1 + \eta_2 \log_2 \eta_2$$

Note that η_1 equals the distinct number of operators, and η_2 equals the distinct number of operands. Therefore:

$$\hat{N} = 9 \log_2 9 \ + 6 \log_2 6$$
$$= 9(3.169) + 6(2.584)$$
$$= 28.521 \ + 15.504$$
$$= 44.025$$

One can next calculate the volume using the following equation:

$$\text{Volume} = \text{length} \times \log_2(\eta_1 + \eta_2)$$
$$= 44.025 \times \log_2 15$$
$$= 171.996$$

The potential volume, V^*, involves a new term, η_2^*, which is defined to be the number of I/O parameters. Thus:

$$V^* = (2 + \eta_2^*)\log_2(2 + \eta_2^*)$$
$$= (2 + 2)\log_2(4)$$
$$= 4\log_2 4$$
$$= 8$$

The boundary volume can also be calculated as follows:

$$V^{**} = (2 + \eta_2^* \log_2 \eta_2^*) \times [\log_2(2 + \eta_2^*)]$$
$$= (4\log_2 2)(\log_2 4)$$
$$= 4(2)$$
$$= 8$$

The level is now calculated:

$$V^* = L \times V$$
$$L = \frac{V^*}{V}$$
$$= \frac{8}{171.996}$$
$$= .0465$$

The level can also be approximated by the equation below:

$$\hat{L} = \left(\frac{2}{\eta_1}\right)\left(\frac{\eta_2}{N_2}\right)$$

Note: N_2 is defined to be the total number of instances of operands.

Thus:

$$\hat{L} = \left(\frac{2}{9}\right) \left(\frac{6}{12}\right)$$

$$= (.222)(.5)$$

$$= .111$$

We can now calculate the intelligence content, I, of the representation:

$$I = \hat{L} \times V$$

$$= .111 \times 171.996$$

$$= 19.09$$

The next four calculations are dependent on the language chosen to implement the algorithm.

1. The programming effort, E, is calculated first and is derived below:

$$E = \frac{V^2}{V*}$$

$$= \frac{(171.996)^2}{8}$$

$$= 3697.828$$

2. The programmer's time, T, is now calculated:

$$T = \frac{E}{S} \qquad \text{where } S = 18$$

$$= \frac{3697.828}{18}$$

$$= 205.434$$

3. The next calculation will involve the language level, λ:

$$\lambda = LV* - L^2V$$

$$= .0465(8) - (.0465)^2 \, 171.996$$

$$= .372 - .3718$$

4. The final language-dependent calculation is defined below:

$$E = \frac{(V^*)^3}{\lambda^2}$$

$$= \frac{8^3}{(.372)^2}$$

$$= 3699.849$$

The next two calculations below involve the estimation of errors.

1. The first of these shows the number of delivered errors, B:

$$B = L \times \frac{E}{E_0} \qquad \text{where } E_0 = 3000$$

$$= .0465 \frac{(3699.849)}{3000}$$

$$= .0465(1.23)$$

$$= .057$$

2. The second calculation is an estimation of the number of errors, $\hat{B}$:

$$\hat{B} = \frac{E^{2/3}}{3000}$$

$$= \frac{(3699.849)^{2/3}}{3000} - \frac{171.996}{3000}$$

$$= \frac{239.215}{3000} = \frac{171.996}{3000}$$

$$= .079$$

or

$$\hat{B} = \frac{V}{3000} = .057$$

Example 2-3   *Analysis of an Exchange Sort program represented in Basic.*

The text of the Bubble Sort algorithm in Basic follows:

```
10    *** EXCHANGE SORT ***
15    REM
20    REM
25    DIM A(10)
30    LET I = 1
35    LET J = 2
40    PRINT "INPUT NUMBER OF ITEMS"
45    INPUT N
50    IF N > 10 GO TO 700
52    PRINT "INPUT";N;"ITEMS"
55    FOR K = 1 TO N
65    INPUT A(K)
70    NEXT K
75    IF A(I) < A(J) GO TO 95
80       LET T = A(I)
85       LET A(I) = A(J)
90       LET A(J) = T
95    LET J = J + 1
100   IF J > N GO TO 115
105      IF J > 10 GO TO 115
110         GO TO 75
115   LET I = I + 1
120   IF I + N GO TO 800
125      LET J = I + 1
130      GO TO 75
700   PRINT "10 IS THE MAXIMUM"
705   LET N = 10
710   GO TO 52
800   PRINT
805   PRINT "ITEMS IN ORDER:"
```

```
810    FOR  K=1  TO  N
815       PRINT  A(K)
820    NEXT  K
999    END
```

The objective is to obtain some indications of the accuracy of some of the formulas used in the software physics. We begin by analyzing the program in terms of the software physics by determining the number of operators (η_1), operands (η_2), and input/output parameters (η_2^*), as well as the total number of occurrences of operands (N_2). It is also assumed here that the speed of mental discriminations (S) is 18, as stated by Halstead (Ha77), for software.

In determining the above, an operand is defined as a variable or some other software element that is operated on. The operator is defined as the elements that perform the operations on an operand. An I/O parameter (η_2^*) is usually an operand also and is counted in both categories. Included in the list of operators (η_1), SEQUENTIAL may be found. The sequential control structure is viewed as operating on the operands in a certain way (i.e., performing steps in sequential order) and is counted as an operand.

(a) OPERANDS

In the case of the sort algorithm in Basic, an array, A, was created, which holds the numbers to be sorted and will eventually hold the sorted numbers. The I and J have been set up as pointers into the array, and T was created as a temporary storage element if a switch of two elements in A is needed. The N was set as an array overflow check to prevent more than ten elements being entered into A, and K is used as an internal counter. Therefore:

OPERANDS

A(array), I, J, $\eta_2 = 6$

K, N, T

(b) I/O PARAMETERS

Of the operands, A and N are considered I/O parameters since each is an input from the user and A is used as the output from the program. Therefore:

<u>I/O PARAMETERS</u>

$$A, N \qquad \eta_2^* = 2$$

(c) OPERATORS

As stated, the SEQUENTIAL control structure is included in this category. Other control structures used are IF.. GO TO and FOR.. NEXT. The assignment control is also used (LET and for =). The INPUT and PRINT statements are used for I/O. The numerical operators >, L, + are also used. Therefore:

<u>OPERATORS</u>

Sequential, Assign(LET, =).

PRINT, INPUT, IF FOR/NEXT, $\qquad \eta_1 = 9$

L, >, +

(d) TOTAL NUMBER OF OCCURRENCES

Here, every reference to A (A(K), A(10), etc.) is counted as well as every physical appearance of an operand. So:

$$N_2 = 34$$

Now, all the necessary components have been collected:

$$\eta_1 = 9 \qquad \eta_2^* = 2 \qquad S = 18$$
$$\eta_2 = 6 \qquad N_2 = 34$$

The simple matter of plugging into the formula remains:

Length: $\qquad \hat{N} = \eta_1 \log_2 \eta_1 + \eta_2 \log_2 \eta_2$

$\qquad\qquad = 9 \log_2 9 + 6 \log_2 6$

$\qquad\qquad = 44$

Volume: $\qquad V = N \log_2 (\eta_1 + \eta_2)$

$\qquad\qquad = 44 \log_2 (15)$

$\qquad\qquad = 172$

Potential volume:

$$V^* = (2 + \eta_2) \log_2(2 + \eta_2^*)$$
$$= (2 + 2) \log_2(2 + 2)$$
$$= 8$$

Boundary volume:

$$V^{**} = (2 + \eta_2^* \log_2 \eta_2^*) \cdot [\log_2(2 + \eta_2^*)] \cdot [\log_2(2 + \eta_2^*)]$$
$$= (4 \log_2 2)(\log_2 4)$$
$$= 6$$

Level:

$$L = \frac{V^*}{V} = \frac{8}{172}$$
$$= .0465$$

Level approximation:

$$\hat{L} = \left(\frac{2}{\eta_1}\right) \left(\frac{\eta_2}{N_2}\right)$$
$$= \left(\frac{2}{9}\right) \left(\frac{6}{34}\right)$$
$$= .0392$$

Intelligence content:

$$I = \hat{L}V = (.0392)(172)$$
$$= 6.7424$$

Language level:

$$\lambda = LV^* = (.0465)(8)$$
$$= .372$$

Effort:

$$E = \frac{V^2}{V^*} = \frac{(172)^2}{8}$$
$$= 3698$$

Time:

$$T = \frac{E}{S} = \frac{3700}{18}$$
$$= 205.5$$

Delivered errors:

$$B = L\left(\frac{E}{E_0}\right) \qquad \text{where } E_0 = 3000$$
$$= .0465 \left(\frac{3700}{3000}\right)$$
$$= .0574$$

Estimated
errors:

$$\hat{B} = \frac{E^{2/3}}{E_0}$$

$$= \frac{(3700)^{2/3}}{3000}$$

$$= .0797$$

or

$$\hat{B} = \frac{V}{E_0}$$

$$= \frac{172}{3000}$$

$$= .0573$$

Example 2-4 *Analysis of an Ada Program*

The following example is part of a buffering task written in Ada:

```
POOL_SIZE : constant : = 100;
  begin
  loop
    select
      when COUNT < POOL_SIZE = >
        accept WRITE(C : in CHARACTER) do
          POOL(IN_INDEX) : = C;
        end;
        IN_INDEX : = IN_INDEX mod POOL_SIZE + 1;
        COUNT
      or when COUNT > 0 = >
        accept READ(C : out CHARACTER) do
          C := POOL(OUT_INDEX) ;
        end;
        OUT_INDEX : = OUT_INDEX mod POOL_SIZE
  + 1;
        COUNT       := COUNT − 1;
      or
        terminate
      end select;
    end loop;
```

(*Note:* Only the main loop is included. The compile time processing of declarations would make them unlikely components of this analysis.)

The first step is to count the total number of distinct operators (η_1) and the total number of distinct operands (η_2).

OPERATORS

$+, =, -, = >, <, >,$ MOD,
terminate, loop, read, write,
select, sequential, rendezvous, $:=$

There are fifteen distinct operators.

OPERANDS

C, 1, 0, 100,
POOL_SIZE, POOL, COUNT,
IN_INDEX, OUT_INDEX

There are nine distinct operands.

The length (N) is then obtained by counting the total usage of η_1 and η_2. For this example:

$$N = 51$$

Using the formula, the appropriate length is as follows:

$$\hat{N} = \eta_1 \log_2 \eta_1 + \eta_2 \log_2 \eta_2$$
$$= 15 \log_2 15 + 9 \log_2 9$$
$$= 87$$

The volume is then found using the values of length found above:

Using Actual Length	Using Approximate Length
$V = 51 \times \log_2(\eta_1 + \eta_2)$	$V' = \hat{N} \times \log_2(\eta_1 + \eta_2)$
$\quad = 51 \times \log_2(15 + 9)$	$\quad = 87 \times \log_2(15 + 9)$
$\quad = 233$	$\quad = 399$

To find the potential volume, the number of input/output parameters (η_2^*) must be known. In our case there is only one, as shown below:

$$V^* = (2 + \eta_2^*) \log_2(2 + \eta_2^*)$$
$$= (2 + 1) \log_2(2 + 1)$$
$$= 4.75$$

The boundary volume is a less idealized lower bound, as follows:

$$V^{**} = (2 + \eta_2^* \log_2 \eta_2^*) \times \log_2(2 + \eta_2^*)$$
$$= [2 + (1)\log_2 1] \times \log_2(2 + 1)$$
$$= 3.17$$

The appropriate *level* of implementation of the algorithm can be obtained from

$$\hat{L} = \left(\frac{2}{\eta_1}\right) \cdot \left(\frac{\eta_2}{N_2}\right)$$

where N_2 = total number of occurrences of operands. In our cases $N_2 = 42$. Thus:

$$\hat{L} = \left(\frac{2}{15}\right) \cdot \left(\frac{9}{26}\right)$$
$$= .0462$$

The *intelligence content* is

$$I = \hat{L} \times V$$
$$= .0462 \times 233$$
$$= 10.76$$

The *programming effort* is given by

$$E = \frac{V^2}{V^*}$$
$$= \frac{(233)^2}{4.75}$$
$$= 11.43 \times 10^3$$

The *programmer's time* is

$$T = \frac{E}{S}$$

where S is the Stroud number and has a value of 18 for software. Thus:

$$T = \frac{22.9 \times 10^3}{18}$$

$$= 635$$

The *language level* is

$$\lambda = L^2V$$

$$= (.0462)^2 \times 233$$

$$= .497$$

This unusually low level is difficult to rationalize except in terms of the fact that some languages have rather large tails in their level distribution (Ha77).

The number of delivered errors can be computed from the following equation:

$$B = L \times \frac{E}{3000}$$

$$= \frac{0.02857 \times 22.9 \times 10^3}{3000}$$

$$= 0.218$$

and the estimated number of errors are computed as follows:

$$\hat{B} = \frac{E^{2/3}}{3000} = \frac{(11.43 \times 10^3)^{2/3}}{3000}$$

$$= .169$$

or

$$\hat{B} = \frac{V}{3000} = \frac{233}{3000}$$

$$= .078$$

2.6 THE BROOKS ESSAYS

The purpose of this section is to review in greater detail the points made by Brooks in *The Mythical Man-Month* (Br75). This volume is a collection of essays on software engineering. It is a valuable collection of experiences derived from the OS-360 software project in which Brooks was project manager. The essays include reports by other specialists as well as reflections on the OS-360 experience.

Brooks notes at the outset that there is a problem of scale in software design and implementation (Br75). He refers to the problem as a "tar pit." He approximates the magnitude of effort associated with a programming product, a programming system, and a programming systems product—relative to a program (see Figure 2–3). He reports roughly a factor of 9 in effort required for a programming systems product compared to a program. He analyzes the phenomenon in terms of "delights and woes" of programming. Many of the woeful aspects of programming turn out to be precisely features of systems and products rather than of programs.

Brooks notes that some of the difficulty in software technology arises from poor estimation or overoptimism. He attributes this phenomenon to the "exceedingly tractable medium" of programming. Programmers have little reason, a priori, to believe that anything will go wrong.

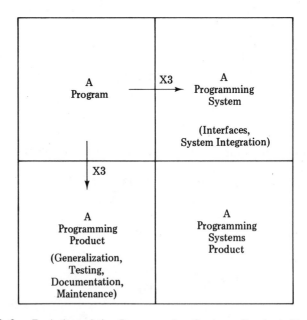

Figure 2-3. Evolution of the Programming Systems Product. (From Br75, p. 5; used with permission.)

He also discusses in considerable detail the noninterchangeability of people and time, thus exposing the "mythical man-month." He notes that some parts of the software life cycle are sequential and cannot be expedited with more people (Br75).

In discussing the life cycle, Brooks suggests a scheduling rule of thumb (Br75, p. 20):

1/3 planning
1/6 coding
1/4 component test and early system test
1/4 system test, all components in hand

If one were to presume that "planning" included requirement statements and software design, then this view of the life cycle is consistent with the Belady and Lehman assertions about where the effort must be placed (BL79).

The problems that emerge when schedules begin to slip have led to the suggestion of Brooks' law:

Adding manpower to a late software project makes it later. [Br75, p. 25].

This "law" arises from the observation that more effort is diverted to training new people for such a project than is realized in new productivity. Brooks concludes that we are left with a "cruel dilemma" between projects that are too large for a few people and those that cannot be expedited by adding people (Br75).

He suggests that the way out of the dilemma is a maintenance of "conceptual integrity" in a piece of software. A number of management techniques are suggested for achieving conceptual integrity. The most profound in relation to current practice is multiple implementation. Here the power of the implementor is limited because of competing products, and as a result the design integrity is preserved. Brooks observes that the use of multiple implementations was a significant feature of the System 360 hardware project but was not used in the OS-360 software project (Br75).

ADDITIONAL EXERCISES

1. Suggest some reasons why the lengths and the length estimates in Examples 2–1, 2–2, and 2–3 do not show the same apparent agreement as in Figure 2–2.

2. Develop a rationale for the use of base-two logarithms in the length operation.

3. Would the programs in Examples 2-1, 2-2, and 2-3 be considered large by the Belady and Lehman criterion? Justify your answers.

4. What counterbalancing factors would make the programming efforts for Exercises 2-2 and 2-3 so close in values?

5. Suppose you were responsible for staffing and training a programming team to produce programs like Examples 2-1, 2-2, and 2-3, develop a policy for diverting personnel to training in the use of higher level tools. Suggest a salary policy that would properly reward the creation of error-free programs.

SUMMATION

The phenomenology of software is a subject that is characterized by interacting psychological observations and direct observations of the object software. So long as there remains a highly creative component in software design, these dual concerns will arise in establishing scientific models. Our observations of the software phenomena suggest that the greatest impact on the design discipline will be achieved in the teaching of appropriate attitudes and disciplines. If the sequel to this chapter is fulfilled, it is quite likely that the observations discussed here will be quite different in the years ahead.

REFERENCES

(BL79)   Belady, L. A., and M. M. Lehman, "Characteristics of Large Systems," *Research Directions in Software Technology*. Cambridge, Mass.: M.I.T. Press, 1979.

(Br75)   Brooks, F. P., *The Mythical Man-Month*. Reading, Mass.: Addison-Wesley Publishing Co., Inc., 1975.

(CC77)   Corbato, F. J., and C. J. Clingen, "A Managerial View of the Multics System Development," *Proceedings of the Conference on Research Directions in Software Technology*. Cambridge, Mass.: M.I.T. Press, 1977.

(De78)   Denning, P. J., "About This Issue," *Computing Surveys*, vol. 10 (1978).

(DLS79) Dyck, V. A., J. D. Lawson, and J. A. Smith, *Introduction to Computing*. Reston, Va.: Reston Publishing Company, Inc., 1979.

(FL78)   Fitzsimmons, A., and T. Love, "A Review and Evaluation of Software Science," *Computing Surveys*, vol. 10 (1978).

(Ha77)   Halstead, M. H., *Elements of Software Science*. New York: Elsevier North-Holland, Inc., 1977.

(Ze78)   Zelkowitz, M. V., "Perspectives on Software Engineering," *Computing Surveys*, vol. 10 (1978).

Requirements
Analysis

3

The purpose of this chapter is to provide an overview of software requirements. Rather than dealing with observations and interpretations of experiments, this chapter and subsequent chapters will focus on specific problems and some of their solutions.

3.1 REQUIREMENTS STATEMENTS

As stated in the previous chapter, requirements statements are descriptions of *what* is to be done as opposed to *how* something is to be done. The motivation behind the study of requirements is an extension of the idea that the first step to solving a problem is understanding the problem. A requirements statement should provide that "understanding of the problem."

As suggested in the discussions of phenomenology, the early stages of the software life cycle are of critical importance in the ultimate performance and economics of the software product. Thus, the intuitive and experimental justification for considering requirements as a part of the life cycle is accepted, although this phase has not attracted a great deal of technical and scientific attention to date. The reasons for this neglect are worth considering at the outset.

One could argue that the case for a requirements statement is self-evident. The problem arises in so many other areas that we can simply borrow from such experiences in other areas. For example, contracts between buyers and sellers in the building or service industries are usually requirements statements as defined above. Failure to negotiate a contract in such cases often leads to the same malaise as failure to prepare requirements for software. Thus, there is a good deal of experience derived from other areas of human activity. Software requirements should thus be considered in differential terms; that is, we should ask: What are the unique features of software that impinge on the contract negotiation process?

EXERCISE 3-1

Prepare a requirements statement for a complete stereophonic sound outfit. Indicate where the requirements are clearly technical and where they are qualitative. Did you use vendor-supplied hardware specifications in preparing the requirements? Why?

In a number of respects, preparing requirements specifications for software is dissimilar to contracting in other areas. First, the buyer and seller are often the same. The software industry is not yet well developed, and the industry that does exist is only a small part of the overall production picture. Traditional software practice involves packaging of hardware and software together. Thus any software that is not a part of the package is usually the responsibility of the buyer.

In large software projects like the OS-360 software, the producer and consumer are the same, at least until the entire system is delivered. The ultimate user is not a party to the requirements specifications. Thus the exclusion of the user is due in part to the fact that the technical know-how to work with the specifications is often available only to the seller.

Furthermore, even if a producer-consumer relationship could be established in one organization, there remain serious difficulties in requirements specifications. As a product, software is difficult to measure both in quantity and quality. Even where the producer is willing to take responsibility for the product, one is never sure whether the responsibility has been met. And given the expected consumer-initiated changes, the responsibility becomes hopelessly obscure.

A part of the difficulty in specifying software derives from insufficient cost data. This aspect of the problem was discussed in Chapter 2. The source of the difficulty, as noted there, is an irrational overoptimism about the cost and effort required to produce software. Seldom does a consumer see a "shopping list" of software parts and prices as one would expect with hardware.

The elusiveness of the product and its costs leads to a secondary problem in managing the requirements activity. How do the parties know that the requirements are well written and complete? Other areas of contracting such as home building, car purchasing, etc., recur so often that a good lawyer can use a standard form with some assurance of its adequacy. The form will have withstood the test of litigation. Since this recurring and tested software experience is not available, the preparation of requirements is often neglected, and the quality is deficient.

3.2 THE IRONMAN EXAMPLE

Before examining some of the existing tools for developing requirements, it is worthwhile to examine an example. A well-known published example of requirements is the IRONMAN specifications for a new programming language (DoD77). The specific features of that language, which are quite controversial, are not at issue here. Rather it is the structure of the requirements documents that is of immediate concern.

One is immediately struck by the care taken in the definition of terms in the IRONMAN requirements:

> A precise and consistent use of terms has been attempted throughout the requirements. Potentially ambiguous terms have been defined in the text. Care has been taken to distinguish between requirements, given as text, and comments about the requirements, given as bracketed notes. [From DoD77]

Since requirements inevitably contain a mixture of absolute necessities and nice things to have, some distinction must be made between levels of necessity. The IRONMAN requirements include a definition of verbs used to describe the priority given an item, as noted below (DoD77):

> The following terms have been used throughout the text to indicate where and to what degree individual requirements apply:

shall	indicates a requirement placed on the language or translator.
should	indicates a desired goal but one for which there is no objective test.
shall attempt	indicates a desired goal but one that may not be achievable given the current state of the art, or may be in conflict with other more important requirements.
shall require	indicates a requirement placed on the user by the language and its translators. (language is subject)
shall permit	indicates a requirement placed on the language to provide an option to the user. (language is subject)
must	indicates a requirement placed on the user by the language and its translators. (user is subject)
may	indicates a requirement placed on the language to provide an option to the user. (user is subject)
will	indicates a consequence that is expected to follow or indicates an intention of the DoD; it does not in any case by itself constrain the design of the language.

These definitions provide a highly visible internal reference to issues that often cause confusion in software design. Where design options and designer creativity do not corrupt the overall integrity, they are explicitly allowed by these definitions.

Areas of a general goal-oriented nature are treated in the "General Design Criteria" section of the IRONMAN specifications. Here issues of "generality," "efficiency," "machine independence," etc., are discussed. The value of this discussion of general design criteria is that where the designer is exercising some freedom, it can be justified on the basis of these criteria. Thus, the requirements become a guiding influence on design decisions.

The remainder of the IRONMAN requirements deals with specific issues related to the language itself. The overall sense of the specific requirements is imperative with numerous uses of "There shall be ...," "The language shall provide ...," etc. The effectiveness of the requirements is indicated by the design progress already achieved (DoD80).

3.3 TOOLS FOR REQUIREMENTS

The IRONMAN example cited in Section 3.2 suggests very clearly that the primary tool for specifying software is prose written in a natural language. This hints at the desperate state of development of this part of the technology and brings to mind John Kennedy's accolade for Winston Churchill on the occasion of awarding the latter honorary U.S. citizenship:

> He mobilized the English language and sent it into battle. (April 9, 1963)

If prose becomes well established as the medium of discourse, the analysis of requirements falls into the more general technical domain of natural language processing. The problems of natural language processing are receiving considerable attention both generally and specifically in the analysis of software requirements. The more general problem is an active area of research within artificial intelligence. Most of the progress has been limited to areas of limited domain of discourse, e.g., elementary foreign language instruction. Software seems, therefore, to be a natural point of significant demonstration of natural language processing. The objective of systematic processing of requirements would be the detection of inconsistencies, contradictions, ambiguities, and incompleteness in the text of the specifications.

A few examples of requirements analysis tools can be cited at this point. The most notable are the ISDOS system developed at the University of Michigan (TH77) and the SREP system under development at TRW. The ISDOS system provides for the ability to write and refine requirements in the same medium. The refinements are ultimately stated in a Problem Statement Language (PSL) where certain primitive concepts are predefined. These primitives include most notably PROCESS, INPUT, OUTPUT, SYNONYM, and EVENT. Qualifiers on the notion of process include USES, UPDATES, and GENERATES, and the objects manipulated include REAL WORLD ENTITIES, SETS, and GROUPS. Once the requirements have been stated in sufficient detail so that the statements conform to the PSL, then a Problem Statement Analyzer (PSA) can produce tables and matrices indicating the structure and consistency of the specifications. By keeping the original and refined versions in the same medium, corrections and incremental analysis are facilitated. The burden of linguistic analysis is on the user, however, since the paraphrasing in the PSL is not automated. An example of the results of the analysis is shown in Figure 3–1, which is an example of a Data Activity Interaction Report. It shows the interaction between data items and processes.

SREP (Software Requirements Engineering Program) is an extension of ISDOS intended to accommodate real-time specifications. Like ISDOS, SREP is composed of a Requirements Statement Language (RSL) and a Requirements Evaluation and Validation System (REVS). Its most notable innovation is the inclusion of automatic generators of simulations from the requirements statements.

In any consideration of tools for requirements statements, one should not overlook direct use of mathematical notation. Stating the mathematical properties of objects and processes helps to capture the essential features and to detect inconsistencies. An example of this point was recently encountered in the design of a degree audit system for a university. Such a system is intended to help monitor a student's progress toward a degree. Degree requirements are usually formulated through committee debates and are stated in English prose. The recognition that degree requirements are *intersections* or predicates defined on the *set* of approved courses and the *set* known as the transcript led to specifying an intermediate language for statements including *set* operations. The intersection algorithm was an obvious candidate for careful analysis and implementation.

The point about the use of mathematics as a tool for requirements specifications will probably seem self-evident to the scientist, but the users and specifiers of new systems are not very often scientists. In typical data-processing applications, mathematical thinking may be quite foreign to many of the participants. It may be as effective for the software group to take a review course of instruction in discrete structures as to take the time to learn a PSL or RSL syntax.

3.4 REQUIREMENTS STATEMENTS AS CONTRACTS

The awareness of the role of legal assistance and contract law in engineering activity is apparent particularly in construction engineering.

```
                            Jul 20, 1982  00:20:52
                    PSL/PSA-Payroll-Example-A5.2

               Data Activity Interaction Report

Data Activity Interaction Matrix


(i,j) value    meaning
----------     ------------------------------------
    R          Row i is received, used or employed by
               column j (input)
    U          Row i is updated by column j
    D          Row i is derived or generated by column j
               (output)
    A          Row i is input to, updated by, and output of
               column j (all)
    F          Row i is input to and output of column j (flow)
    1          Row i is input to and updated by column j
    2          Row i is updated by and output of column j



                        8 terminating-emp-processing --- /
                       7 process-library ------------- /
                      6 payroll-processing ---------- / |

                 5 new-employee-processing ------ /
                4 employee-processing ---------- / |
               3 employee -------------------- / |
              2 departments-and-employees ---- / |
             1 departments ----------------- / |
                                            | | | | | | | |
    -----------------------------------------+---------+------+
     1 employee-forms ----------------       |         |      |
     2 employee-information ---------         |  D      |  R   |
     3 employment-termination-form --         |         |      R
     4 tax-withholding-certificate --         |  D   R  |      |
     5 time-card -------------------          |  D      |      |
                                            +---------+------+
     6 employee-reports ------------          |         |      |
     7 error-listing ---------------          |         |      |
     8 hired-employee-report --------          |      D  |      |
     9 pay-statement --------------          |  R      |      |
    10 paysystem-outputs -----------          |  R      |  D   |
                                            +---------+------+
    11 terminated-employee-report ---          |         |      D|
    12 department-file --------------          |         |      |
    13 employment-forms-archive -----          |         |      |
    14 hourly-employee-file ---------          |         |      |
    15 job-code-file ----------------          |         |      |
                                            +---------+------+
    16 projects-file ----------------          |         |      |
    17 salaried-employee-file -------          |         |      |
    18 skill-file -------------------          |         |      |
    19 system-database --------------          |         |      |
    -----------------------------------------+---------+------+
```

Figure 3-1.   An Example of a Data Activity Interaction Report. (Reprinted from Te82, p. 68.)

Similar concerns with regard to software have been slow to emerge largely because of observations already discussed in Chapter 2, such as the difficulty in measuring software and the difficulty in estimating the cost of software. As with any newly emerging industry, the issues of patent rights and copyrights are not yet adequately defined, so there is no real protection of ownership. Even the question of whether the software industry is a service or product industry is yet to be resolved. All these concerns notwithstanding, firms and individuals still enter into contracts for the delivery of software.

Accepting the fact that contract law has evolved out of a need to solve problems that have only strained analogs in the software industry, the basic principles do, nonetheless, suggest some guidelines. First, the contract must be entered into by competent persons. Amongst these persons there must be a definite promisor and promisee (DY71). The principle of requiring competent persons covers the obvious exclusion of such persons as infants, mental incompetents, and the intoxicated. But it is not unusual to find that one party to a software contract may be viewed as incompetent relative to the other. Thus it is fair to observe that the greatest difficulty in negotiating software requirements emanates from the disparity in technical knowledge between the parties to the agreement.

Contracts are further weakened because software is seldom delivered as a finished "turn key" product. The delivery is usually made over a period of time, after cooperative design activity on the part of all parties. Thus, the identification of a promisor and promisee is often very difficult. There have been some attempts to define "systems responsibility" with attendant consideration for the buyer if delivery is not made on time. However, such a practice often incurs much higher contract costs because of the risk to the seller.

In general, a contract must deal with definite and legal subject matter. The issue of definiteness (or the lack thereof) has already been discussed and illustrated in Chapter 2. The issue of "legal subject matter" is also clouded by the primitive nature of the patent and copyright laws as they are applied to software.

The role of *acceptance and offer* and the need for a contract to be supported by *financial consideration* are so universal that they would apply as well to software as to any other contracting activity. The size of the financial consideration is quite another issue and is fraught with all those difficulties associated with estimating the cost of software.

In spite of all of the difficulties cited here, there is appearing a glimmer of light in a mode of contracting that is quite analogous to commissions for works of art. Here the parties may be definite as to their role and clearly competent. The contract may involve stages of delivery, any one of which could be the last. As the project progresses from the more creative phases to the more mundane, the basis of consideration may change from cost plus fixed fee to a competitively based fee schedule. Many recent defense and space system projects have had such characteristics. A good example of a system still evolving through such a scenario is the U.S. Army's Tactical Computer System. The design and prototype construction have been handled by a single contractor who has been very responsive to changing requirements and test results. The system will soon enter into a production phase wherein bidding will be a part of the scene again. The unfortunate part of such an arrangement is that the original developer is often left with a fully elaborated design based on obsolescent technology. The new entries into the production competition will have the advantage of the design work without being tied to the technology.

Software, like any other engineering and design activity, can be and is the subject of contracts. The application of old and tried rules as well as the recognition of the need of phased contracting seems to be the most workable policy in writing contracts.

REFERENCES

(DoD77)   Department of Defense, "Requirements for High Order Computer Programming Languages," *Sigplan Notices,* vol. 12 (1977).

(DoD80)   Department of Defense, *Ada Programming Language,* 1980.

(DY71)   Dunham, C. W., and R. D. Young, *Contracts, Specifications, and Law for Engineers.* New York: McGraw-Hill Book Company, 1971.

(Te82)   Teichroew, D. "Problem Statement Language (PSL), Problem Statement Analyzer (PSA), Example," ISDOS Project, Univ. of Michigan, 1982.

Software Design

4

Software design is a natural extension of the refinement processes that are applied to requirements. The objective is to segment the software into manageable portions where manageability includes considerations of implementation and maintenance. The distinction between requirements and design is difficult to define precisely, but at the point of selection of logical data structures most would say the activity is design. Thus, the software and data tend to take on structure during the design process.

The most prominent issue in software design is the criterion to be used in giving the software structure. Such a criterion not only would guide the human activity of design but would also determine the possibilities of verifying that the design conforms to the requirements. The problem of verification is sufficiently pervasive that it could be argued that it motivates all of software technology.

The earliest recognition of the software structure problem was evidenced by interest in *modular programming,* a term that was used to describe programming in small pieces. It was approached as a management issue with the objective of improving the productivity of each programmer. In this primitive stage, there was little recognition of technical issues associated with program segmentation.

The awareness of software design as a part of the technology was heightened by the pioneering work of P. L. Parnas on modularization (Pa72). He noted that quite different structure is obtained when different criteria are used to segment software. He proposed a criterion called "information hiding" wherein one attempts to hide each design decision from all other decisions. The result is a structure that conforms more to the design decision structure than to the logical structure of the ultimate program.

EXERCISE 4-1

List the important design decisions that would be encountered in developing a program to play chess. Suppose one module arises from the decision to represent the chessboard as an array. What operations or subroutines would become part of the module? What subsequent decisions would determine the next subordinate level of modular structure?

Most notable subsequent developments in design technology have been extensions or refinements of Parnas' ideas. Criteria for judging the quality of a modularization have been proposed by W. P. Stevens, G. Myers, and L. L. Constantine in a paper titled "Structured Design"

(SMC74). These authors propose a grading scheme based on "cohesion levels" and "coupling levels." Cohesion levels are used to indicate the extent to which the module adheres to a unified purpose. Coupling levels apply to pairs of modules and indicate the extent of interaction between them. The levels and their definitions are given in Tables 4-1 and 4-2.

TABLE 4-1

COHESION LEVELS

In order of decreasing desirability

---

1. *Informational*
   This type of module has multiple entry points, each with a single function associated with it. All functions are related through a shared object, concept, or resource. This type of cohesion was the objective of the Parnas "information hiding" modularization.

2. *Functional*
   This type of module performs a single function (e.g., square root).

3. *Communicational*
   This type of module performs a sequence of functions all of which are related by data or resource usage (e.g., copy a file).

4. *Procedural*
   This type of module performs a sequence of functions where the sequence is required (e.g., data plotting).

5. *Classical*
   This type of module performs several functions in sequence, but the sequencing is incidental (e.g., initialization or termination).

6. *Logical*
   This type of module contains several related functions, one of which is selected by each invocation (e.g., error message printing).

7. *Coincidental*
   This type of module either has no functional description or is composed of multiple completely unrelated functions. The modularization might be achieved by using scissors on a flow chart or program listing.

TABLE 4-2

COUPLING LEVELS

In order of decreasing desirability

---

1. *Data Coupling*
   The modules pass homogeneous or scalar data items between each other.

2. *Stamp Coupling*
   The modules pass nonhomogeneous items or too much data for the function being performed (e.g., passing an entire personnel record in order to update the annual income).

(Continued)

3. *Control Coupling*
   As perceived by the invoker, an element of control is passed between modules. The element of control may be passed up or down in the subordinate structure. One of several functions may be selected in the module being invoked.

4. *External Coupling*
   The coupled modules share global variables. Each module must use the same names for the variables.

5. *Common Coupling*
   The coupled modules share a global resource, but common names or attributes are not required.

6. *Content Coupling*
   One module contains direct references to the insides of another. The references may be to code or to local environment.

The design methodology proposed by Stevens, Myers, and Constantine (SMC74), and later separately by Myers (My75) and L. L. Constantine and E. Yourdon (YC79), is viewed as an extension of documentation techniques such as HIPO (St76) and structured programming (DDH72). All of these authors proposed a graphical representation of software structure, one that is intended to capture the extent of coupling and cohesion. For example, the following "structure chart" indicates two modules, A and B, where B is subordinate to A (i.e., A invokes B).

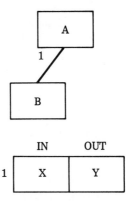

The invocation involves a formal parameter, X (a name in A), and a value returned, Y (a name in A). As variations on the form of coupling, the modules may not be subordinate one to the other, as shown here:

Or the modules may share environments:

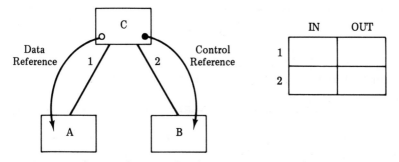

By way of example, consider the structure of a stack manipulation module shown here:

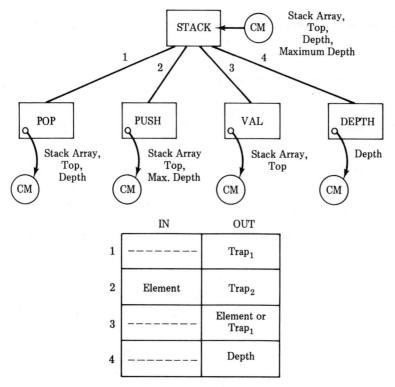

This specification of the stack module focuses on the interfaces with subordinate modules. The modules exhibit *common coupling* in this specification, and the subordinates Pop, Push, Val, and Depth have functional cohesion since only one function is being performed.

(*Note:* The "traps" in this example are control coupling variables which force some action upon the parent module. The form "exception" is synonymous with "trap").

EXERCISE 4-2

Convert the STACK module given above into a single module with informational cohesion. How does this form alter the user's viewpoint in invoking a stack manipulation?

Acknowledging that software design technology is still developing and that the notation is far from universally accepted, the subsequent sections will elaborate on some of the dominant threads of thinking today.

Example 4-1   A Garbage Collection System

The problem is to modularize a garbage collection algorithm. See Figure 4-1(a) and (b). An algorithm of this type is mainly seen in an operating system to recover lost resources, i.e., memory. The lost resources are those that are unable to be used by the system for any reason.

In this problem one has to deal with a source memory, M, which is to be cleaned up, and an allocatable memory, A, which is the compacted data. We are dealing with only list structures with this module. Each memory location will contain a type, datum, and link, where type is defined to be an atom, list, or garbage. The datum is defined to be a value, a pointer to a list, or a pointer to A. A queue is used if a list is found inside a list. Finally, our initial conditions are m, which is the starting position in M; a, which is the next position in A; and the queue is initially empty.

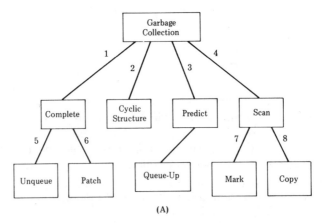

(A)

Figure 4-1   (a) Structure of the Garbage Collection Module. (*Continued*)

IN   OUT

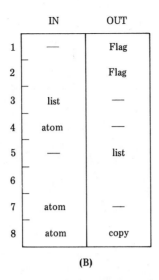

	IN	OUT
1	—	Flag
2		Flag
3	list	—
4	atom	—
5	—	list
6		
7	atom	—
8	atom	copy

(B)

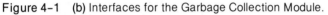

Figure 4-1   (b) Interfaces for the Garbage Collection Module.

The complete module is used for checking the queue and patching memory. It is invoked when m = nil. The cyclic structure is used when the type of m is garbage. It then sets m to nil, which triggers the complete module. The predict module is used when the type of m is a list. The list is queued for future processing. The scan module is used to move atoms from M to A, (i.e. copy), and to mark m garbage.

This design uses functional cohesion within the modules. It also exhibits control coupling.

Example 4-2   Design of a Text Editor

The problem is to modularize a text editor. The text editor should have the capability to allow full screen edit. See Figure 4-2(a) and (b).

The pager module allows one to view any full screen of text beginning at a line number specified by the user. The keyboard module is used to move the cursor. Single characters can be retyped at the point of the cursor. The move module is a destructive move of a block of test to a target location. It is inserted at the target location. The delete module is used to delete a block of text specified by the user and concatenates the remaining text. The copy module is similar to the move module, but the source is not destroyed. A target location and block of text are specified by the user. The add module is used to append new text to the current text. The new text is placed at a target location specified by the user. The find module is used to search the text to find the first occurrence of a character string specified by the user.

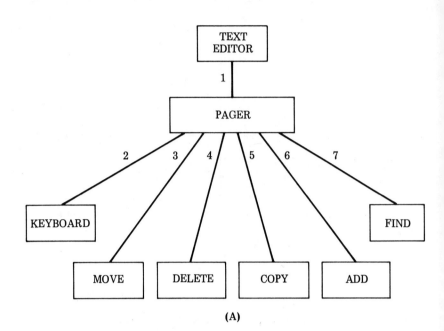

(A)

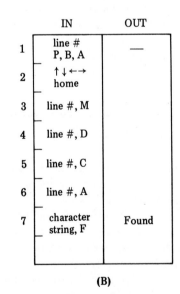

(B)

Figure 4-2 (a) Overall Structure of a Text Editor. (b) The Interface Components of a Text Editor.

The design uses functional cohesion and can be further refined; i.e., the insert that replaces all occurrences of x with y can be subordinate to the add module. Stamp coupling is evident in that each module is passed a complete copy of text for manipulation.

4.1 OBJECTIVES OF SOFTWARE MODULARIZATION

Stated simply, any design methodology must be capable of reducing the complexity of the object or system to human proportions. Even in the conventional design methodologies such as physical structures, the systems modularization (supports, plumbing, electrical, etc.) tends to reduce the complexity of that which is being implemented at any one time. The design methodology may be founded on fundamental principles of physics, which tends to ensure that critical interfaces behave properly. Thus, to extend the analogy, the interfaces between systems in physical structures may involve insulation, spacings, grounding, expansion allowances, etc. The principles are sufficiently fundamental that they are readily understood outside of the particular context of application.

The objectives of software design remain very much the same, namely, the reduction of complexity. The laws governing the interfaces are not so well understood, and what laws have been proposed cannot be regarded as "laws of nature." The designer has little choice but to minimize the interfaces between the pieces of the software. The objective of reducing the complexity of software becomes implicitly an objective of reducing the interaction between the pieces.

The medium of design must also be considered in an analysis of objectives. For instance, in structures, the design objective may be to create "detailed blueprints." The medium itself becomes part of the design product. The medium must achieve a balance between specifying the design and allowing some flexibility in achieving an implementation. The medium should also encourage verification by inspection of the final product. This is a feature that is often overlooked in software design methodologies. To use the analogy of a building again, with blueprint in hand, one should be able to identify in which room one is standing and whether that room conforms to the design constraints (i.e., number of windows, placement of electrical outlets, type of flooring, etc.). The design medium must capture not only the designer's intent but must also in a sense be a model or idealization of the real thing.

This dual role of the medium immediately opens the side issue of software documentation. In becoming a model of a piece of software, the design in a sense documents the properties of the software. As the implementation evolves, and as maintenance is undertaken, it is reasonable to suggest that the design medium must also evolve into a documentation medium. In a similar fashion, blueprints become important documents in the maintenance of a building and may even be redrawn as changes are made.

In general terms the objective of software design may be thought of as the reduction of complexity in a software product through the minimization of interaction between the parts. The medium of design should express the design decisions and should support verification and maintenance of the final product.

Other concerns that emerge in the application of a design methodology include:

Size: Even in conceptually simple computations, size is a source of complexity from the point of view of implementation and maintenance.

Commonality: The design methodology should lead to the identification of "off the shelf" parts.

Programming tools: The design should express structures that are achievable with extant programming tools. For example, the means of implementation of a module is typically the subroutine, but the designed structure (the module) and the program structure (the subroutine) are often incompatible.

4.2 TOOLS OF SOFTWARE DESIGN

As noted in the introduction to this chapter, there has been some development of design tools of a graphical nature. The design is represented as nodes and interconnecting edges with appropriate annotations. The graphical tools tend to capture the hierarchical structure of software, but they leave many of the design objectives unattended. In particular, the desired effect of the module should be formalized in the design process, and the medium should be a model of the final product. What is needed is a tool that can represent varying levels of detail from the first attempt at decomposition down to the final coded realization. With this requirement, the design tools would become extensions of both common flow-charting techniques and programming language notations. The current state of the art is best illustrated by the succession of steps each using different tools as shown in Figure 4–3.

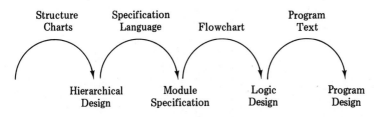

Figure 4-3.   The Sequence of Tools Commonly Used in Software Design.

The design objectives would be best served by a single medium that allowed ever finer detail in the specifications, i.e., analogous to the use of "scale" in blueprints (see Figure 4-4).

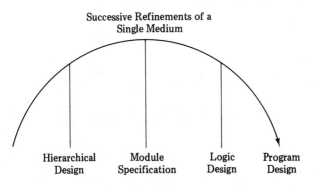

Figure 4-4.   Successive Refinements of a Single Medium.

The technological experience with software suggests a few properties that a design medium should have:

1. The module interface specifications must be in the module prologue. This requirement recognizes that interfaces are specified in the prologue of program text.
2. Structure charts, flow charts, and program components must be subsets of the design components.
3. The medium must allow naming of components in a way that the names are meaningful in the final program.

Recognizing that structure charts, flow charts, and programs are easily specified through rectangular contours, the only new component to be described is the module. Each module would include at most an interface prologue, exceptions, logic, and effect. The following graphics would meet the objective:

Module

(A)

Module with an
Interface
Prologue

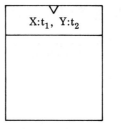   return t_3

t_3 is the type of the value produced, and
X and Y are formal parameters of type t_1
and t_2 respectively.

(B)

The Complete
Module

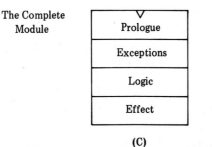

(C)

In the completely elaborated module, the exceptions and effects may be formal mathematical specifications of the domain and mapping, respectively, of the function to be computed. They may appear as comments in the final program, or they may be critical program components in a language such as Euclid.

The example of the previous section is repeated here to illustrate the use of the design notation; see Figure 4–5(a)–(e).

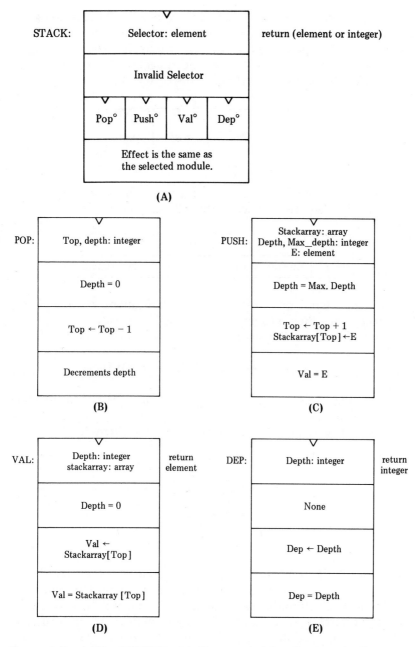

Figure 4-5.   (a) The STACK Module Represented As a Rectangular Contour. (b) The POP Module.   (c) The Push Module.   (d) The Val Module.   (e) The *Depth* Module.

The same hierarchical structure is presented below, but additional detail is readily visible. First, control coupling between the using module and STACK is apparent in the "selector" parameter. The choice of one of the functions is apparent in the logic design. (The ° notation is borrowed from the Jackson design methodology (Ja75).

▽	▽	▽	▽
Pop°	Push°	Val°	Depth°

It means select one of the items at this level. This same logic section could be detailed even further by the following figure:

Case Selector of			
Pop( )	Push (Element)	Value ← Val( )	Value ← Depth( )

This figure tends to provide more specifications on the actual parameters and their meaning. In the imbedded functions, Pop, Push, Val, and Depth, the specifications include program elements such as

$$VALUE \leftarrow STACKARRAY\ [TOP]$$

Thus, all the levels of detail and refinement are included in the same design medium.

The structure of the module box as proposed here is:

It is taken rather directly from proposals made by Parnas (Pa72) and Robinson et al. (Ro77), and as such is not an innovation. The imbedding of the module within the logic part and freely mixing the graphics for modules and logic are the key to the integrity of this approach to design. The notion of "module" is carried to any level of detail. The appearance of a module in a design is a signal that coupling issues are paramount in reducing the complexity at that point. The appearance of a logic component is an indication that algorithmic complexity is crucial to the design, and the appearance of program components would indicate that implementation efficiencies are being considered.

The proposed software design tools will be summarized here in order to illustrate the rigor of the syntax and to avoid ambiguities in subsequent examples. Two fundamental processes (specification and invocation) arise in using the rectangular contours; see Figure 4-6(a) and (b). Within the "logic" part of the specification, several levels of detail are possible, but if additional modularization is to be shown, the processes diagrammed in Figure 4-7(a)–(e) are useful.

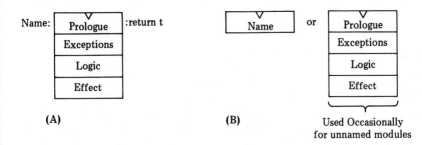

(A)   (B)   Used Occasionally
                          for unnamed modules

Figure 4-6 (a) Specification.   (b) Invocation. (Used occasionally for unnamed modules.)

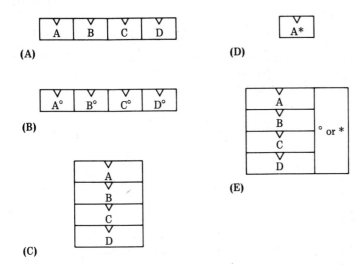

Figure 4-7 (a) Subordination. (No logic is implied.) (b) Selection. (c) Rough sequencing. (d) Iteration. (e) Extended Selection and Iteration. (Rough sequences may be selected or repeated.)

4.3 THE PROCESS OF DESIGN

The process by which the tools are used to achieve the design objectives will ultimately influence the integrity of the design as much as the tools. By "process" we mean the mental steps taken in splitting and interconnecting the modules. Many times these mental steps arise quite unconsciously from the structure of the data or from the function being performed. It is useful, however, to place some labels on the processes so that they may be recognized and similarities may be exploited.

Myers (My75) has proposed a list of design processes that can be clearly identified in the methodology. His list of processes includes the Source/Transform/Sink Decomposition, the Transaction Decomposition, and the Function Decomposition.

The Source/Transform/Sink Decomposition is based on the data flow through the software. The best known example of the decomposition is the typical programming language compiler (see Figure 4-8 and Section 6.2). The evolution of this structure was the product of many pressures including limitations in the earliest hardware hosts. The structure arises often enough that one might ask how it might be obtained intentionally. Myers suggests a process of data abstraction wherein the Source produces a distinctly different structure from the input, and the Sink accepts a structure clearly distinguished from the output (My75). The decomposition is made at the first point in the data transformation (coming from the ends) where this clear distinction exists. Thus, an abstracted form of the input and output data is handled by the Transform part of the decomposition. Maintaining the points of decomposition at the extremes tends to maximize the cohesion of the Source and Sink modules. It is worth noting, in light of the discussion in the previous section, that any of the processes discussed here may be repeated and imbedded. Thus, the Transform module (the parser in Figure 4-8), for example, may be further decomposed using the same Source/Transform/Sink process.

The process of Transaction Decomposition is utilized whenever a module is to select one from a number of subordinates. The example of the STACK module in the previous section illustrates the result of this

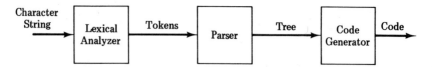

Figure 4-8.   Design of a Typical Compiler.

process. The decomposition can be viewed as based on data value rather than on data type as in the Source/Transform/Sink Decomposition. The data value is considered to be a control value. Thus this type of modularization arises when modules are control coupled. The decomposition is illustrated by the design of a general data management system (see Figure 4-9). The top level in Figure 4-9 is an example of Source/Transform/Sink Decomposition. The "master" module is further decomposed into transaction modules. One or more of these transactions would be selected on the basis of control information passed from the interpreter.

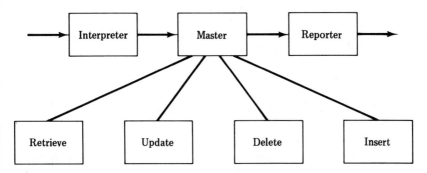

Figure 4-9.   Design of a Typical Data Base Management System.

In the case of a Function Decomposition process, the new modules arise out of stepwise refinement of the logic design. As each contained function is identified, a data coupling to it may be established, and that function is designed on the basis of imposed specifications. This is perhaps the purest form of decomposition since it tends to lead to the most desirable coupling and the highest level of cohesion. Consider for instance the design of a search module shown in Figure 4-10. The

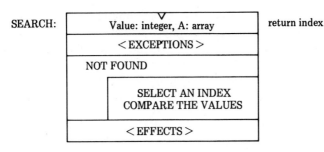

Figure 4-10.   Decomposition of a Search Module.

search module contains at least two possible imbedded modules: "select an index" and "compare the values." One of the primary justifications and motivations for Function Decomposition arises from the relative ease in propagating verification arguments. As an example, in the simplest case of

$$F(G(X))$$

where some postcondition, R, must be met, the corresponding weakest precondition, WP, is

$$WP(G, WP(F,R))$$

(See Chapter 5 for a thorough discussion of this methodology.) It is noteworthy that Function Decomposition is a basic process in deriving the preconditions.

4.4 PACKAGING OF SOFTWARE

Although much of the existing design methodology leads to the packaging of modules as subroutines, it is important to keep the packaging issue quite separate. The dominant design issue is the control of intermodule interface complexity, and there are several ways of doing this.

Any discussion of packaging ultimately returns to the issue of high-level versus low-level languages. Even the lowest level of programming system will often provide a packaging feature for software modules. For instance, some microprogrammable machines provide CALL and RETURN instructions, which provide for saving and recovering microcode addresses at one level of imbedding. Most macrofacilities are low-level means of substituting a module into each place it is invoked. More advanced macrofacilities may also provide parameter substitutions within the module.

At the other end of the scale, programming systems are now under development that package software modules within data definitions. Languages such as ALPHARD (Wu77) use the data typing facility to control the complexity of the module interfaces involved. The development of path expressions (Ha77) may also be viewed as a step toward limiting the complexity of interfaces between synchronized parallel processes.

For the commonly available high-level programming systems, the subroutine (procedures) and the "block" seem to provide the most convenient packaging for modules. In such structures the user is provided with explicit controls over the environment of the module and a means of specifying the interface through parameters. It has been stylish to allow so many defaults in the interface specifications, however, that the complexity easily gets out of hand simply by leaving things out. It is also fair to observe that the "value returned" mechanism in many programming languages is very limiting, especially if the value is a composite one (i.e., an array, list, or string).

If a software designer wishes to adopt a packaging discipline independent of that which is imposed by the implementation language, some consideration should be given to Dijkstra's proposal (Di76) on the scope of variables. He suggests a discipline wherein every variable to be used in a block (or module in this context) must be declared therein. The scope is divided into an "active" and "inactive" scope based on the viability of the value associated with a variable.

Example 4-3   *Design of a Text Editor Using Rectangular Contours*

This example will illustrate the use of rectangular contours; see Figure 4-11 (a)–(h). The text editor of Example 4-2 will be used in this example.

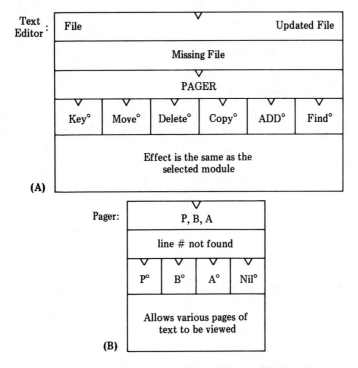

Figure 4-11 (a) Overall Design of a Text Editor. (b) The Pager Module. (*Continued*)

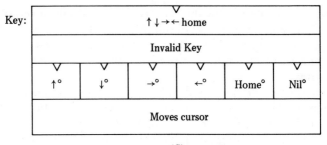

Key:

↑ ↓ → ← home
Invalid Key

↑°	↓°	→°	←°	Home°	Nil°

Moves cursor

(C)

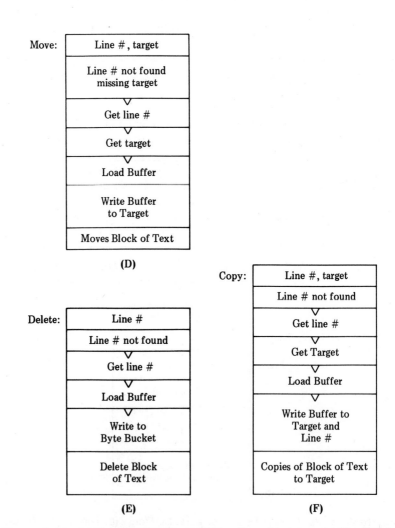

Move:

Line # , target
Line # not found missing target
Get line #
Get target
Load Buffer
Write Buffer to Target
Moves Block of Text

(D)

Delete:

Line #
Line # not found
Get line #
Load Buffer
Write to Byte Bucket
Delete Block of Text

(E)

Copy:

Line #, target
Line # not found
Get line #
Get Target
Load Buffer
Write Buffer to Target and Line #
Copies of Block of Text to Target

(F)

Figure 4-11   (c) The Key Module.   (d) The Move Module.   (e) The Delete Module.   (f) The Copy Module. (*Continued*)

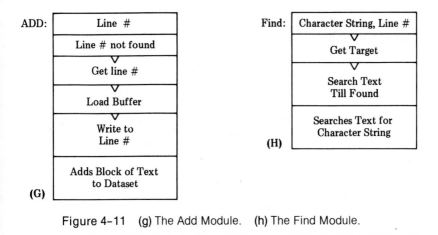

Figure 4-11   (g) The Add Module.   (h) The Find Module.

Example 4-4   *Design of a Symbol Table Manager*

The purpose of this example is to illustrate the use of the software design techniques of Sections 4.2 and 4.3 in the design of a symbol table management module. Symbol table management is a key element of language processors, and as such this example is a small part of the larger case study considered in Section 6.2.

The symbol table management activity can be thought of as two inverse functions—lex and image (see Figure 4-12).

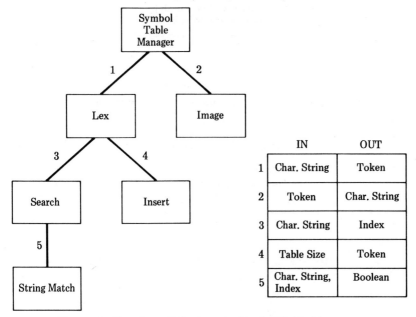

Figure 4-12.   Overall Design of a Symbol Table Manager.

The same design represented in rectangular contours would appear as shown in Figure 4–13(a)–(f).

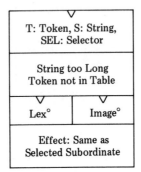

(A)

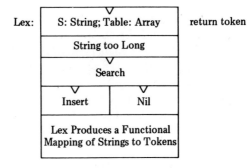

(B)

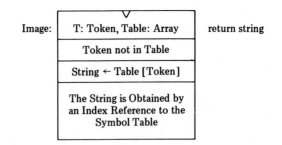

(C)

Figure 4-13 **(a)** The Symbol Table Manager in Rectangular Contours. **(b)** The Lex Module.   **(c)** The Image Module. (*Continued*)

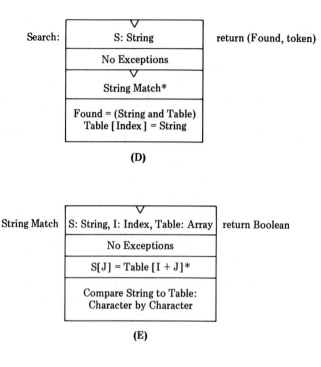

(D)

(E)

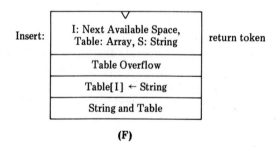

(F)

Figure 4-13   (d) The Search Module.   (e) The String Match Module.   (f) The Insert Module.

The compactness of the structure charts is evidently of value in capturing a snapshot of the design. The rectangular contours, on the other hand, provide for design specifications and variable levels of detail in the partial logic part.

Example 4-5   A Chess Board Analysis Module

This program is designed to calculate the length of move (LOM) of a number of chess moves and the average LOM (AVGLOM) for all the moves. Also each move will be determined to be either a ROOK, BISHOP, or KNIGHT move (TYPE). The total number of occurrences of each type of move and the total number of moves are also given.

The program realizes the chessboard as an 8×8 matrix:

31	32	33	$\cdots$
21	22	23	$\cdots$
11	12	13	$\cdots$

The chess moves are coded by a FROM number and a TO number. Each of these is a two-digit number in the range (inclusive):

11 to 18
21 to 28
31 to 38
.
.
.
81 to 88

If a coordinate is entered outside the above ranges, the entry is flagged as an illegal move and is not counted in any calculations even though it is listed. Also, the program will flag an impossible move (i.e., impossible by a single move or a single piece) as an illegal move. For example:

FROM	TO	LOM	TYPE
11	28		Illegal move
-34	56		Illegal move
91	21		Illegal move
.			
.			
.			

A legal move takes on the following form:

FROM	TO	LOM	TYPE
11	31	2	ROOK
33	88	5	BISHOP
32	44	2	KNIGHT

A KNIGHT move is assumed to be of length 2. Actually two interpretations exist in which a KNIGHT move could be either 2 or 3, as shown below:

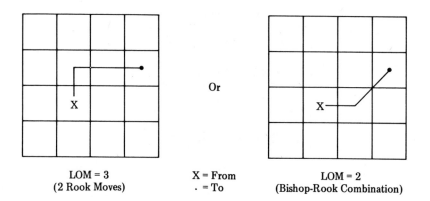

| LOM = 3 | X = From | LOM = 2 |
| (2 Rook Moves) | . = To | (Bishop-Rook Combination) |

The second move (LOM = 2) is assumed here.

The program calculates the LOM and TYPE by breaking the coordinates of the FROM and TO entry into four components and performing a subtraction:

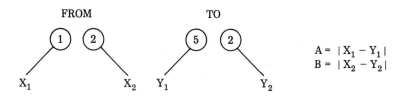

$$A = |X_1 - Y_1|$$
$$B = |X_2 - Y_2|$$

and by following the logic that

$$ROOK = (A \text{ or } B = 0) \wedge \left(LOM = \begin{Bmatrix} A \text{ if } B = 0 \\ B \text{ if } A = 0 \end{Bmatrix}\right)$$

$$BISHOP \equiv (A = B) \wedge (LOM = A \text{ or } B)$$

$$KNIGHT \equiv (A = 1) \wedge (B = 2) \text{ or } (A = 2) \wedge (B = 1) \wedge (LOM = 2)$$

The type and LOM can be determined if none of the above conditions is true (at this point the coordinates have been checked for range violations) the if entry is impossible by a single move of a single piece and is flagged ILLEGAL; see Figure 4–14(a)–(f).

Move Analyzer: 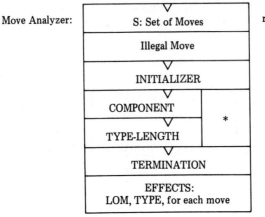 return (Table of move
Types and
Average Length)

(A)

INITIALIZER: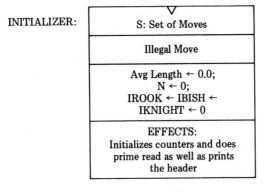

(B)

COMPONENT: 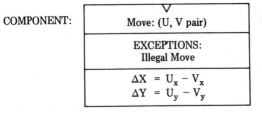 return (ΔX, ΔY)

(C)

Figure 4-14 (a) The Move Analyzer Module. (b) The Initializer Module.
(c) The Directional Component Module. (*Continued*)

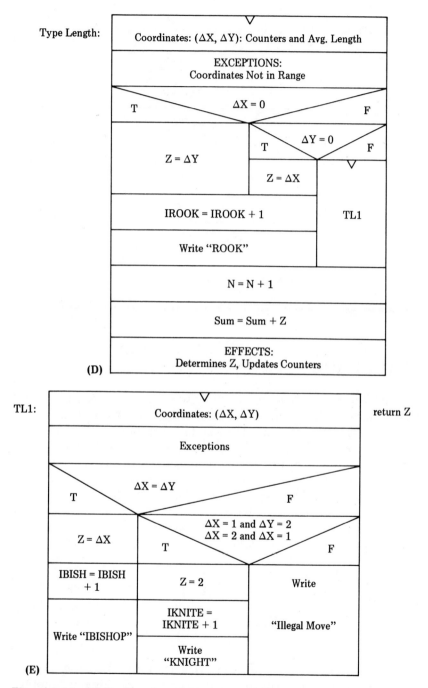

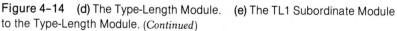

Figure 4-14   (d) The Type-Length Module.   (e) The TL1 Subordinate Module to the Type-Length Module. (*Continued*)

TERMINATION: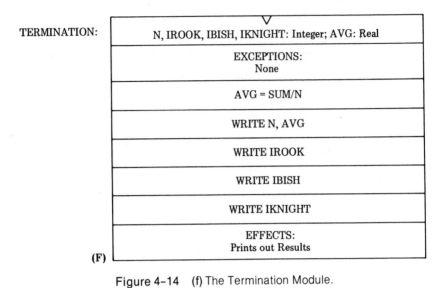

Figure 4-14   (f) The Termination Module.

4.5 ADA AS A SOFTWARE DESIGN LANGUAGE

As noted in the previous sections, the issue of packaging of software has been addressed by adapting facilities and linguistic structures that were designed for other purposes. The adaptation of subroutines and macros for the representation of software modules is a classic case. In the former, a control structure is used to design environment and interface features of software. In the case of macros, the crucial interface structures are often highly stilted and devoid of generality.

The programming language Ada is the first all-new language design to emerge since the issues of software design have been well understood. Thus, it is instructive to consider the role that Ada may play in design methodology.

Ironically, the packaging of software is handled in Ada (DoD80) by a structure known as the "package." Syntactically the package is a declaration in the same sense that data types and subroutines are declarations. However, packages, subprograms, and tasks are also separately compilable, which gives packages, in particular, some very useful visibility properties.

The Ada package consists of two parts: the package specification and the package body. The specification part provides interface information only, whereas the package body contains the completely elaborated definition of the items in the package. The specification part is often referred to as the "visible" part, thus implying that the body is invisible. The relevance of the package for "information hiding" (Section 4.1) is apparent. The invisibility of the body is readily enforced by the separate compilability feature. The implementor may provide to the user the name of the compilation unit through the "program library" without disclosing the details of the definition.

The stated purpose of the package is to bring together logically connected components of a program such that their maintenance may be pursued as a single unit. The consideration of cohesion is evident from such use. The interfaces between components of the packages and other program components are handled as in any other parameter definition. Thus, no special features are included for defining the mathematical properties of the interfaces (note exception and effects in Section 4.2).

The now familiar example of the definition of a "stack" will be pursued again as an example of Ada packages:

```
package STACK is
    procedure POP;
    procedure PUSH (X:element);
    function VAL return element;
    function DEPTH return integer;
end STACK;

package body STACK is
    STACKARRAY: array (0..255) of element;
    MAX_DEPTH: integer: = 256;
    TOP: integer: = - 1;
    procedure POP is
    begin
      if top = - 1 then
        exception
      else
        top: = top - 1
      end if;
    end POP;
```

```
procedure PUSH (X:element) is
begin
  top: = top + 1
  if top = max__depth then
    exception
  else
    stackarray [top]: = x
  end if;
end push;

function VAL return element is
begin
  if top = - 1 then
    exception
  else
    return stackarray [top]
  and if;
end VAL;

function DEPTH return integer is
begin
  return top + 1
end DEPTH;
end STACK:
```

The user of such a design of the STACK may acquire the visible components (i.e., POP, PUSH, VAL, and DEPTH) by writing:

with STACK;

.

.

.

within the declaration part of some other program. Furthermore, the operations may become directly visible by subsequently writing

use STACK;

in some declarative part.

(*Note:* In the above example of the STACK package, the definitions of "element" and "exception" were intentionally unspecified. The former is readily handled through the "generic" facility of Ada. Exceptions have special structures for their definition and "raising" in the language as well.)

In addition to the modularization and information-hiding role of Ada packages, such packages also provide a linguistic structure that closely models the theoretical notion of *type*. A *type* is defined to be a set of objects and a set of operations that are applicable to the objects [e.g., integers and (add, subtract, and multiply)]. Many predecessor languages provided controls over the set of objects by allowing constraints to the stated. However, Ada permits the gathering of the operations and the type declaration into a package. In so doing, by declaring the type to be "private" or "limited private," the applicable operations are constrained to be those procedures and functions specified in the same package. The distinction between "private" and "limited private" is that the former allows equal, unequal, and assignment as operations whereas "limited private" does not.

The package specification for the STACK can thus be reconstructed as shown below:

```
package STACK is
    STACK__TYPE is limited private;
    procedure POP (S: stack__type);
    procedure PUSH (S: stack__type, X: element);
    function VAL (S: stack__type) return element;
    function DEPTH (S: stack__type) return integer;
    private
        type STACK__TYPE is array (0..255) of element;
end STACK;
```

Note that the stack body would also be changed by replacing uses of "stackarray" by uses of the formal parameter "S." The declaration of STACKARRAY would be eliminated, and the user would be obliged to declare

Y: stack.stack__type

and, subsequently, to use Y only as a parameter to the procedures and functions in the STACK package.

SUMMATION

Software design stands out as a critical bridge between informal require-ments statements and the rigor of programming methodology. In its cur-rent state of development, it is based on very general principles such as "information hiding," and "a picture is worth a thousand words." No standard medium of design has emerged even though the features of such a medium are now well understood. In the traditional practice of software design and implementation, nothing is more prevalent than the lack of attention to design. Asking a software engineer for blueprints is likely to lead to a presentation of volumes of code, or even worse, to a paranoid explanation of the pressures of schedules and deadlines. The creation and maintenance of software design documentation, whatever the medium, are key elements to avoiding many of the pitfalls cited in Chapter 2.

REFERENCES

(CY75)   Constantine, L. L., and E. Yourdon, *Structured Design*. New York: Yourdon, Inc., 1975.

(DDH72)   Dahl, O. J., E. W. Dijkstra, and C. A. R. Hoare, *Structured Program-ming*. New York: Academic Press, Inc., 1972.

(Di76)   Dijkstra, E. W., *A Discipline of Programming*, Chap. 10. Englewood Cliffs, N.J.: Prentice-Hall, Inc., 1976.

(DoD80)   U.S. Department of Defense, *Military Standard Ada Programming Language*, MIL–STD–1815, December 10, 1980.

(Ha77)   Habermann, A. N., "On the Concurrency of Parallel Processes," *Perspectives on Computer Science*. New York: Academic Press, Inc., 1977.

(Ja75)   Jackson, M. A., *Principles of Program Design*. New York: Academic Press, Inc., 1975.

(My75)   Myers, G., *Composite/Structured Design*. New York: Van Nostrand Reinhold Company, 1978.

(Pa72)   Parnas, D. L., "On the Criteria To Be Used in Decomposing Systems Into Modules," *Communications of the ACM*, vol. 15 (December 1972).

(Ro77)   Robinson, L., et al., "A Formal Methodology for the Design of Operating System Software," *Current Trends in Programming Methodology*, vol. I. Englewood Cliffs, N.J.: Prentice-Hall, Inc., 1977.

(St76)   Stay, J., "HIPO and Integrated Program Design," *IBM Systems Jour-nal*, vol. 15 (1976).

(SMC74)   Stevens, W. P., G. Myers, and L. L. Constantine, "Structured Design," *IBM Systems Journal*, vol. 13 (1974).

(Wu77)   Wulf, W. A., "Some Thoughts on the Next Generation of Programming Languages," *Perspectives on Computer Science*. New York: Academic Press, Inc., 1977.

(YC79)   Yourdon, E., and Constantine, L. L., *Structured Design*. Englewood Cliffs, N.J.: Prentice-Hall, Inc., 1979.

Programming
Methodology

5

Stated loosely and informally, programming methodology is the study of processes and tools used by the programmer when working alone. The condition—working alone—is a recognition of a situation where most of the interface issues with other tasks and programmers have been resolved. Presumably, the programmer has a well-specified and isolated task to be accomplished.

Once again, analogies can be found in other design and engineering activities. The final fabrication of a machine part from blueprints and the installation of building materials both present convenient examples. As F. P. Brooks (Br75) observed, the greatest distinction in the case of programming is that the medium is deceptively tractable. The design problems arise from mental shortcomings on the part of the programmer rather than from material deficiencies.

The design issues to be addressed in programming center around the choices of representations of algorithms and data. The representations are ultimately to be realized in correct program text ready for compilation and execution.

In the context of software technology, programming methodology is, like design, a process oriented toward and motivated by verification concerns. The methodology has developed as a means of constructing correct programs "naturally." Reasoning about programs is also an important part of the methodology. Some tools exist in the methodology for producing convincing arguments about the validity of a program.

As noted in the discussion of the software experience (Chapter 1), the development of the methodology was highlighted by the pioneering works of E. W. Dijkstra (Di68), (DDH72), and (Di76). In the first of these contributions, Dijkstra suggested that the methodology should involve the use of those few program building blocks that support the reasoning process. The proposition, stated simply, was that programming should use the IF..THEN..ELSE, DO..WHILE, and SEQUENTIAL controls as building blocks. Independent theoretical work has sustained the completeness of these components in the sense that all programs expressible in other terms could be expressed using these so-called structured controls (BJ66). There has also been extensive development of inference techniques based on the building blocks (Mi75), (Wi73).

The development of programming methodology has progressed along two, not altogether distinct, paths. On the one hand, techniques and language features have been developed that enhance the visualization of critical properties of a program. Even without formal verification facilities, these techniques tend to enhance the chances of producing correct programs. In this area of development would be included everything from Dijkstra's "stepwise refinement" proposal (DDH72) to the very mundane considerations of program formatting and indentation.

On the other side of the methodology is the activity in development of inference systems for programs (programming logic). This has emerged as perhaps the most fertile area of research in theoretical computer science. This work has included the development of specialized induction techniques such as structural induction (Bu69) and the study of program invariants in terms of fixed-point properties (Ye77).

5.1 THE PROGRAMMING PROBLEM

It is useful in a discussion of programming methodology to keep in mind what the problem really is. The technology and science are both oriented toward solving the *automatic programming* problem. It is recognized at the outset that the automatic programming problem is very difficult and may never be solved, or it may not have a solution (because of inherent decidability limitations). Loosely, the automatic programming problem may be viewed as in Figure 5–1.

That is, given the desired state of computation (the postcondition) and the initial state of computation (the precondition), what is the program? We know enough about programming to know that the solution of a programming problem is often not unique. Of the possible solutions, there are obviously differences with regard to superfluous components. One could usually add $X \leftarrow X$ to a program without changing its properties with respect to the conditions given. This situation arises because the conditions may be too weak to eliminate such solutions. Even more likely, there may be an implied condition that the solution be "minimum" in some sense. However, even if the solutions are minimum ones, there may remain several practical realizations of the program. The differences may arise in data representation, iterative or recursive control, or the set of supporting primitive operations. Here again, strengthening the conditions may eliminate some solutions, but such a process may

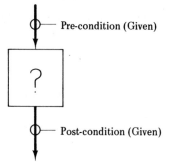

Figure 5-1. The Programming Problem.

also inadvertently eliminate the "best" solution if the trade-offs are not well quantified. The classical time-space trade-off is one of the most vexing in this regard.

The solution to the automatic programming problem is justifiably a dream of every computer scientist, but until its realization, programs must be written and problems will be solved with the aid of programs. Thus it behooves every programmer to become familiar with heuristic approaches to the problem.

5.2 STATES OF COMPUTATION

Since the notions of pre- and postconditions have already arisen in this discussion of programming methodology, it is worth pausing to elaborate upon the meaning of such conditions. The purpose of these conditions is to describe the state of computation at a particular point in a program. In everyday terms, the conditions are equivalent to the specification of coordinates on a two-dimensional space, as shown below:

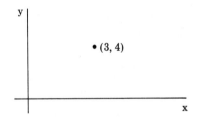

The *state vector*, X, is a pair:

$$X = \begin{bmatrix} x \\ y \end{bmatrix}$$

and the *state* at the given point is described by the *condition*

$$X = \begin{bmatrix} 3 \\ 4 \end{bmatrix}$$

This condition limits the state to single point. The condition may be weaker than the stated one, thus allowing more points to be included in the state specification. For instance, the following specification

$$||X|| \leq 5$$

would admit all points on or within the circle of radius 5 centered at the origin.

The analogy between the above example and *states of computation* is direct and straightforward. We may regard the *environment* of a program as being the equivalent of the *state vector*. Thus, all of those variables, data structures, types, devices, and operations that are "known" at the point in question constitute the state vector. Our ability to place conditions on the state vector is largely determined by the features of the language being used to control what is "known." To say an object is known at some point of a computation is equivalent to saying that it is subject to manipulation and/or inspection.

The extremes of language capability with respect to controllability of the state vector are (1) the machine language and (2) the scope proposals by Dijkstra (Di76). In the former and most primitive case, the state vector is the collection of memory elements (i.e., bits) that are accessible in the machine. In Dijkstra's proposal, however, there is no implicit environment for any program segment. Instead, the programmer must mention every variable to be used by a segment (block) even if its origin is global.

5.3 HEURISTIC REASONING ABOUT PROGRAMS

The first, and perhaps the most profound, step toward heuristic program construction is achieved by weakening the precondition:

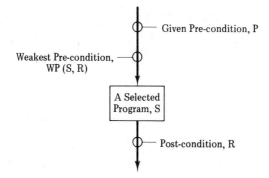

The reasoning about such a program follows the pattern:

1. Select a likely program component, S.
2. Derive the weakest precondition, WP(S,R), for this program component and the given postcondition. (This derivation is supported by a "calculus" of programs that will be discussed later.)
3. Prove that P implies WP(S,R). If this can be proven, then the state of computation will satisfy R after the completion of S.

The program construction process involves *select, derive,* and *prove.* The selection is heuristic in that we have some reason to believe it works. The derivation of the weakest precondition involves some well-defined rules for predicate transformations [i.e., transforming the predicate, R, into WP(S,R)]. The notion of weakest precondition is such that it defines the largest set of states of computation such that starting from any state in the set, the program, S, *will terminate* in a state satisfying R.

The notation and intricacy of the definition of the weakest precondition should not obscure the fact that it is a *condition* that constrains the state of computation. It may be used like any other condition in reasoning about the program at hand.

5.4 STEPWISE REFINEMENT

Our ability to carry out the heuristic reasoning just illustrated is determined by the availability of the *predicate transformer.* The predicate transformers for several simple program components are known, and the process of composing conditions is fairly well understood. Thus, to reason about a program we must begin with small segments. The decomposition of a programming task into small pieces is an important and key step in the methodology. The "top-down," "stepwise refinement" proposals by Dijkstra (DDH72) were intended to address this decomposition problem.

In the stepwise refinement process, one attempts to organize program components by identifying the subordinate parts in such a way that their function is kept simple and is easily verified. These subordinate parts will in turn have parts that are subjected to the same methodology. Ultimately, the program is described in terms of the "primitive" operations of a language or virtual machine. No further refinement is possible on these primitive components. The process is an extension of the Function Decomposition process that was mentioned in the chapter on software design (Chapter 4).

The stepwise refinement process can be illustrated by considering the problem of reversal of a sequence of items, e.g.:

$$(1, \ 2, \ 3) \ \rightarrow \ (3, \ 2, \ 1)$$

At the topmost level we might describe the computation as

```
Reverse:  array A[1:N]
          for I: = 1 step 1 until ⌊ N/2 ⌋ do
          exchange A[I] with A[N + 1 − I]
```

Two components of this version stand out as needing further refinement. First, the expression $\lfloor N/2 \rfloor$ is now commonly used to mean "the next lower integer" from N/2. The $\lfloor \quad \rfloor$ notation is borrowed from APL and is read "floor." Second, the "exchange...with" expression requires further elaboration. The only refinement achieved at the top level is the specification of the array, A, and the use of iteration to traverse the array. A single data structure and the dominant control structure for traversal make this a nearly ideal degree of refinement at any one level.

Proceeding to the next level, the floor operation might be achieved by

$$\lfloor x \rfloor \; : \; \max k$$
$$k \le x$$

or

$$\lfloor x \rfloor \; : \; k := 0$$
$$\text{while } k < x \text{ do} \quad k := k + 1$$
$$\text{return } k\text{-}1$$

Once again, a new data object, k, and an iteration have been introduced at this level of refinement.

Furthermore, the "exchange ... with" expression may be refined by

$$\text{Exchange x with y:} \quad \text{begin } T := x$$
$$x := y$$
$$y := T$$
$$\text{end}$$

Here a single data object, T, is introduced, and a sequence of control is specified for its use. This expression could be further refined by specifying the meaning of the subscripts. However, subscripting is usually a primitive operation in higher-level languages. Thus, no further refinement would be called for.

The refinement process can be viewed as the evolution of a tree from the top down:

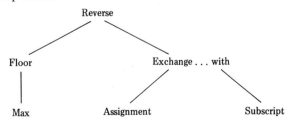

In its purest form, the process proceeds from the top down to those functions that are expressed in terms of primitive concepts. In practice,
however, the process is seldom workable in its purest form. As one proceeds along apparently independent branches of the tree, one encounters common or nearly common substructures. Rather than repeat
the design for each branch, the programmer is led very naturally to some
bottom-up design to build some useful tools. In effect, a new virtual
machine is created that becomes a new target for the top-down process.
Since the new machine was not available in the early stages of the top-
down refinement, those parts may have to be redesigned. Thus, the
refinement process is most realistically viewed as an iteration of top-
down and bottom-up designs.

5.5 MENTAL AIDS IN REASONING ABOUT PROGRAMS

The discussion about stepwise refinement of programs was presented in
a form devoid of *conditions* to be met by the various states of computation. It must not be forgotten, however, that the process was motivated
by the need to reason about the program. Given that the components
are now "well structured" in the sense that the preconditions may be
derived, one must also account for some reasoning techniques that apply
to the refined components.

At each stage of the program development, one would attempt to
state conditions that capture only the essential features of the computation at that point. This is the process of *abstraction*. It leaves the details
of the next step of refinement unspecified, and thus the details become
the product of ingenious selection on the part of the programmer.

There are specific situations in reasoning about programs where
the derivation of weakest preconditions may be augmented with other
logical aids. For example, in the case of a conditional structure, the given
precondition, P, may first be propagated through the test, B. Thus:

$$Q_1 : \text{P and B}$$
$$Q_2 : \text{P and not B}$$

where Q_1 and Q_2 apply at points shown in Figure 5–2. Then the usual
process of select, derive, and prove would be applied to *both* S_1 and S_2.
The following would be proven:

$$Q_1 \implies \text{WP}(S_1, R)$$

and

$$Q_2 \implies WP(S_2, R)$$

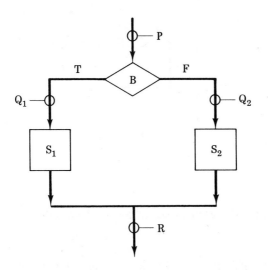

Figure 5-2. State of Computation in a Conditional Structure.

The process being utilized is an example of *enumeration*. That is, in this case, all of the options are exhaustively analyzed.

Iteration and recursion also present cases where additional mental aids are helpful. Here the notion of *induction* is of some utility. One reasons about a base case (i.e., the 0th case); then one proves the same condition for the $n+1$ th case given the condition for the n th case. The inductive inference is that the condition holds for all n.

The most common example of the induction process is the reasoning about *loop invariants*. Consider the case of the WHILE. . DO schema (see Figure 5–3). Suppose that it can be shown that

$$P \implies Q \text{ (the 0th case)}$$

Then if it can be shown that

$$Q \text{ and } B \implies WP(S, Q) \qquad (n\text{th} \implies n+1\text{th case})$$

we know that Q is true for all n; that is, Q is a loop invariant. One final step completes the enumeration:

$$Q \text{ and not } B \implies R$$

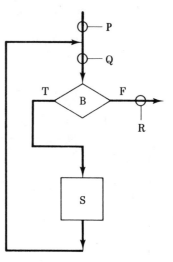

Figure 5-3.   State of Computation in a WHILE. . DO Structure.

The construction of the loop invariant is so important in this process that it tends to overshadow the inductive reasoning involved. Indeed, the line of reasoning gives very few clues about how to construct the loop invariant. There have been several formal attempts at solving this problem (BM75), but a very simple rule of thumb seems to work quite well as a start. Considering the final step in the proof

$$Q \text{ and not } B \implies R$$

one might expect to construct Q by relaxing the "not B" condition from R. Since R is given, and since it usually includes a statement of completion, the *relaxation* step is usually straightforward.

The issue of proper termination also arises in the case of iterations and recursions. A most useful reasoning aid for proving termination is the *well-founded set*. Such a set has a starting element, t_0, and all the elements have the property that

$$t_k > t_j \qquad \text{for all } k > j$$

If the states of computation can be functionally converted (mapped) to elements of such a set, and if:

The initial state maps to t_N,
Each loop or recursion decreases t, and
The loop of recursion stops for t_0,

then termination is assured. Quite often an iteration will have an index that has all the properties of the well-founded set (i.e., the nonnegative integers). Otherwise, a new variable might be introduced to include this set as a component of the state of computation.

5.6 WEAKEST PRECONDITIONS AND HEURISTIC REASONING ABOUT PROGRAMS

The suggestion of a calculus of programs based on derived weakest preconditions for program components immediately raises the question of how notions of loop invariants and well-founded sets relate to the derivations. The connection can be illustrated by starting with the WHILE..DO construct (see Figure 5–4). Its semantics are represented as

$$WP((WHILE..DO),R) = \exists\ k:\ k \geq 0:\ H_k(R)$$

where $H_k(R)$ is the weakest precondition that the state, R, will be reached in k or fewer steps. Thus,

$$H_k(R) = [B \wedge WP(S,H_{k-1}(R))]\ \text{or}\ [\neg B \wedge R]$$

$$H_0(R) = \neg B \wedge R$$

The derivation of $H_k(R)$ would require a tedious enumeration of each step around the loop.

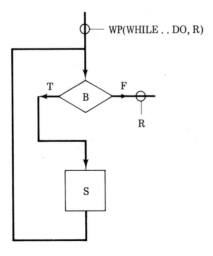

Figure 5-4.   The WHILE..DO Structure.

One is then left with the question of whether the weakest precondition can be strengthened such that this enumeration is avoided. Thus we would like to know the properties of Q_1 such that

$$Q_1 \text{ and Termination} \Rightarrow \text{WP(WHILE..DO,} Q_1 \wedge \neg B)$$

The "termination" condition may also be written as

$$\text{Termination} = \text{WP(WHILE..DO,T)}$$

The role of Q_1 can be seen in Figure 5-5.

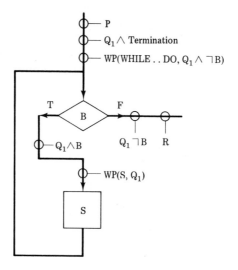

Figure 5-5. The Loop Invariant in a WHILE..DO Structure.

It can be shown that if

$$Q_1 \wedge B \Rightarrow \text{WP(SP,} Q_1)$$

then Q_1 will have the desired property. Stated simply, it is sufficient that Q_1 be a *loop invariant*. The idea behind the reasoning process is to find a Q_1 that is as weak as possible and still be invariant. See Figure 5-6.

Figure 5-6. The Weakening of the Loop Invariant.

EXERCISE 5-1

Prove that if

$$Q_1 \wedge B \implies WP(S, Q_1)$$

then Q_1 and Termination $\implies WP(WHILE..DO, Q_1 \wedge \neg B)$.
A similar proof can be found in Di76.

One might further incorporate the termination condition in Q_1 (thus strengthening it even more) and ask under what conditions does

$$Q \implies WP(WHILE..DO, Q \wedge \neg B)$$

(*Note:* This is a new, stronger Q; see Figure 5-7.) Here again the invariance condition is part of the restriction

$$Q \wedge B \implies WP(S, Q)$$

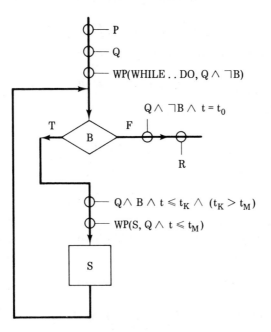

Figure 5-7.   State of Computation in a WHILE..DO Structure.

In addition, it will be required that

$$Q \wedge B \ \Rightarrow \ t > t_0$$

and

$$Q \wedge B \wedge (t \le t_K) \wedge (t_K > t_M) \ \Rightarrow \ WP(S, t \le t_M)$$

for some K,M where t is the mapping of the state to a well-founded set. The t_K, t_M, and t_0 are elements of the well-founded set, t_0 being the minimum element.

All that is left from the previous exercise is to show that under the stated restrictions (i.e., sufficient conditions),

$$Q \ \Rightarrow \ \text{Termination}$$

or equivalently,

$$Q \ \Rightarrow \ WP(\text{WHILE}..\text{DO},T)$$

The proof relies on an intermediate proof that

$$Q \wedge t \le t_K \ \Rightarrow \ H_K(T)$$

This can be proven inductively by observing that for $K = 0$,

$$Q \wedge t (\le t_0) \ \Rightarrow \ H_0(T) \ = \ \neg B$$

but by definition of t_0, we see that

$$t \le t_0 \ \Rightarrow \ t = t_0 \ \Rightarrow \ \neg(t > t_0)$$

Restating the $K = 0$ case, we have

$$\neg Q \vee t > t_0 \vee \neg B$$

which is the same as

$$Q \wedge B \ \Rightarrow \ t > t_0$$

the second restriction. Thus, the $K = 0$ case is affirmed.

Combining the invariance condition (the first restriction) with the third restriction gives

$$Q \wedge B \wedge (t \le t_K) \wedge (t_K > t_M) \ \Rightarrow \ WP(S, Q \text{ and } t \le t_M)$$

Assume that the desired result is true for M. Thus:

$$Q \wedge B \wedge (t \leq t_K) \wedge (t_K > t_M) \ \Rightarrow \ WP(S, H_M(T))$$

Also

$$Q \wedge \neg B \wedge t \leq t_K \wedge (t_K > t_M) \ \Rightarrow \ \neg B$$
$$= \ H_0(T)$$

Combining these results to eliminate the B and $\neg$ B, we have

$$Q \wedge (t \leq t_K) \wedge (t_K > t_M) \ \Rightarrow \ WP(S, H_M(T)) \vee H_0(T)$$
$$= \ H_{M+1}(T)$$

Also note that

$$Q \wedge t \leq t_{M+1} \ \Rightarrow \ (Q \wedge t \leq t_K \wedge t_K > t_M)$$

which by transitivity of the implications is

$$Q \wedge t \leq t_{M+1} \ \Rightarrow \ H_{M+1}(T)$$

This completes the inductive proof.

Since t is a finite function of the state, we have

$$\exists k: \ k \geq 0: \ t \leq t_K$$

When combined with Q, this gives

$$Q \ \Rightarrow \ \exists k: \ k \geq 0: \ t \leq t_K \wedge Q$$
$$\Rightarrow \ \exists k: \ k \geq 0: \ H_K(T)$$
$$= \ WP(WHILE..DO, T)$$

The conclusion is that the restrictions are sufficient to ensure that the loop terminates.

As one final observation, this line of reasoning about the WHILE..DO loop left the computation in a state described by

$$Q \wedge \neg B$$

Thus the original problem of showing that

$$P \ \Rightarrow \ WP(WHILE..DO, R)$$

is replaced by several problems as listed in the following page:

1. Find a suitable Q.
2. Find a suitable well-founded set.
3. Prove that $P \Rightarrow Q$.
4. Prove that $Q \wedge \neg B \Rightarrow R$.

The logical connection between the results developed above is shown in Figure 5–8. Thus, the process of developing the loop invariant and the well-founded set may be viewed as strengthening the weakest precondition. Such a process will tend to eliminate some of the allowable starting states. The given precondition, P, would necessarily be more restrictive.

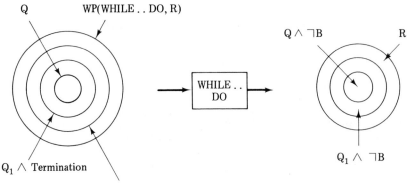

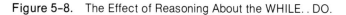

Figure 5–8.   The Effect of Reasoning About the WHILE.. DO.

5.7 MAKING ASSERTIONS ABOUT PROGRAMS

Given the program refinement techniques and given the mental aids in reasoning about programs, there remains a problem of *getting started* in the reasoning process. Getting started involves making useful assertions about the program and about representations of objects and concepts in the program. This problem has been treated in part in the previous chapters on requirements and design. Much of that discussion was oriented toward developing formal statements about the behavior of the resulting programs. For the purposes of this discussion, we will assume that the design process has been successful in generating formal specifications. In practice, this point is reached only through iteration between design and programming.

Even if the pre- and postconditions are well formulated, there will be additional assertions to be made about the program under construction. These arise in the form of *axioms,* which describe the properties of computational and data objects. Such axioms have already been encountered in the discussion of mental aids. In illustrating the enumerative and inductive reasoning processes, the inferences made about the state of computation, such as

$$P \text{ and } B \Rightarrow WP(S_1,R)$$

and

$$P \text{ and not } B \Rightarrow WP(S_2,R)$$

for the conditional structure, may be viewed as axioms on that structure.

In order to complete the axiomatic basis for programming methodology, the four primitive computations of *skip, abort, assignment,* and *sequencing* need specification. Consider as axioms:

$$WP(\text{Skip},R) = R$$
$$WP(\text{Abort},R) = F$$

In the former, it is understood that "skip" or equivalently "no-op" does not admit any states to R that are not already in R. Thus, if the initial state is in R, then the final state will also be in R. The "abort" component is one that does not allow the computation to reach the final state. Thus, there are no states that leave the computation in R.

It is useful to extend the "skip" axiom to include "pure expressions"; thus:

$$WP(\text{pureexp},R) = R$$

Pure expressions are those that are free of *side effects* in that there are no assignments or device changes. Such expressions exist in programs as environment references (i.e., a simple mention of a variable), or as data object references (i.e., A[i,j]). In actual computations, the concept of pure expression is only an approximation since there are usually assignments to a clock and local registers as the computation proceeds. Thus R must be expressed in terms of a restricted form of symbolism such as occurs in most programming languages in order for the pureexp axiom to hold. The pureexp property is usually presumed for boolean expression, B, in

It is a matter of good programming practice to avoid side effects in boolean expressions being used for control purposes.

The familiar assignment statement in programming requires its own axiom for deriving the weakest precondition. If the postcondition to an assignment such as

$$X \leftarrow e$$

is R (e is an arbitrarily complex expression), then the weakest precondition is R with all occurrences of X in R replaced by e. Thus,

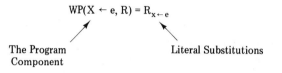

$$\text{WP}(X \leftarrow e, R) = R_{x \leftarrow e}$$

The Program   Literal Substitutions
Component

A few elementary examples illustrate the process and its intuitive correctness. Consider first the assignment of a constant:

$$\text{WP:} \quad \{(C = C) \quad \} \equiv \text{WP:} \quad \{\text{True}\}$$
$$X \leftarrow C$$
$$R: \quad \{X = C\}$$

That is, if the requirement after the assignment is that X = C, then the weakest precondition is "true." Thus all initial states produce the desired outcome.

In a similar fashion, consider the question of whether the program shown in Figure 5–9 will compute the minimum of A, B, C for all initial states. Note that

R: {X ≤ A and X ≤ B and X ≤ C and (X = A or X = B or X = C)}

By enumerative reasoning the following conditions can be derived:

1. A ≤ B
2. B < A
3. A ≤ B and A ≤ C
4. A ≤ B and C < A
5. B < A and B ≤ C
6. B < A and C < B

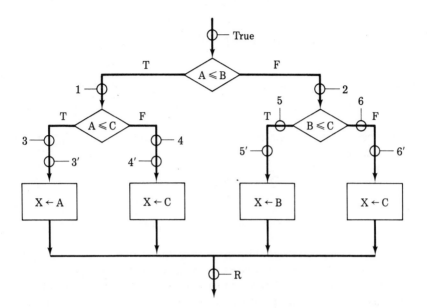

Figure 5-9. Program for the Minimum of A, B, and C.

The weakest preconditions for each of the assignments are obtained by substitution:

3. $A \leq A$ and $A \leq B$ and $A \leq C$
4. $C \leq A$ and $C \leq B$ and $C \leq C$
5. $B \leq A$ and $B \leq B$ and $B \leq C$
6. $C \leq A$ and $C \leq B$ and $C \leq C$

One must now show that

$$3 \Rightarrow 3' \text{ and } 4 \Rightarrow 4' \text{ and } 5 \Rightarrow 5' \text{ and } 6 \Rightarrow 6'$$

which is a straightforward step utilizing only a transitivity property of the ordering relation $<$.

One last primitive computational structure, *sequencing*, also requires axiomatic treatment. Here, it is presumed that the weakest precondition is derived by function composition:

$$WP(S_1;S_2,R) = WP(S_1,WP(S_2,R))$$

The reasoning process can be illustrated with the "exchange ... with" program segment discussed in Section 5.4, as shown in the following page:

$$P: \quad \{x = x' \text{ and } y = y'\}$$

exchange x with y: begin T: $= x;$ $\leftarrow$ ①

$$x: = y; \quad \leftarrow \quad ②$$

$$y: = T \quad \leftarrow \quad ③$$

end

$$R: \quad \{x = y' \text{ and } y = x'\}$$

Applying the assignment axiom three times and the sequencing axiom twice produces

$$③ \quad : \{x = y' \text{ and } T = x\}$$

$$② \quad : \{y = y' \text{ and } T = x'\}$$

$$① \quad : \{y = y' \text{ and } x = x'\}$$

The reasoning is completed by observing that P => 1 .

These axioms and the related mental aids play such a profound role in heuristic program construction that they can be viewed as forming a *calculus* of programming. In this view, the weakest preconditions are *predicate transformers*. Programming is a process of selection of appropriate predicate transformations. The predicate transformers are also a description of the semantics of the programming language. Thus, the burden is upon the language implementer to be sure that the program segments carry out state transitions according to the calculus. Likewise, the burden is upon the programmer to use only those program components that are well formed in the calculus.

Dijkstra (Di76) has extended this notion of a calculus of programs to include nondeterministic components. Here, the conditional and iterative structures are replaced by "alternative" and "repetition" in the form:

$$\text{IF} \quad B_1 \rightarrow S_1 \quad \square$$
$$B_2 \rightarrow S_2 \quad \square$$
$$\cdot$$
$$\cdot$$
$$\cdot$$
$$B_n \rightarrow S_n \quad \text{FI}$$

and

$$\text{DO} \quad B_1 \rightarrow S_1 \quad \square$$
$$B_2 \rightarrow S_2 \quad \square$$
$$\cdot$$
$$\cdot$$
$$\cdot$$
$$B_n \rightarrow S_n \quad \text{OD}$$

For the alternative structure, one of the true B_i's is selected, and the corresponding S_i is performed. If all the B_i's are false, the alternative aborts. The repetitive structure repeatedly selects one of the true B_i's and performs the corresponding S_i. When all the B_i's are false, the repetitive DO..OD statement is completed.

These components, known generically as *guarded commands*, have the advantage that unnecessary sequencing tends to be eliminated from the program, thus simplifying the reasoning process. Dijkstra has extended the calculus to include these nondeterministic structures. He proposed the weakest preconditions:

$$WP(IF,R) \text{ and } WP(DO,R)$$

and he illustrates their use in program construction (Di76).

One step in abstraction above the axioms of programs and their associated calculus the programmer must deal with assertions about data. Assertions about data are, like other structures, the starting point for reasoning about the program. The distinction in the case of data is that the assertions are subject to more design choices. T. A. Standish has proposed a few *ground axioms* for data that deal with fundamental notions of reference, assignment, and construction (St78). The design of a *data type* is determined by how new assertions are generated from the ground axioms and how these assertions are grouped together. The notion of data type is very close to the notion of module in software design. A number of related functions are brought together, and axioms are used to describe their effects. The actual representation or realization of the data is hidden from the user of the functions.

Employing the notation developed by J. V. Gutlag, E. Horowitz, and D. R. Musser (GHM78), one might specify a list as follows:

```
List[any]
    declare  CAR(LIST) → any
             CDR(LIST) → LIST
             CONS(ANY,LIST) → LIST
    for all LϵLIST and xϵAny
        ISLIST(Null)
        CAR(CONS(x,L)) = x
        CDR(CONS(x,L)) = L
    end
```

The assertions bracketed by for all ... end serve two distinct roles. First, they are design specifications for CAR, CDR, and CONS. Second, they are axioms that may be used in reasoning by anyone using the list type. It is the latter use that is of great interest in programming methodology. A collection of such designs and specifications for familiar data structures may be found in GHM78.

Unfortunately, one of the most familiar data structures, the array, admits a variety of designs and thus a variety of "axiomatizations." One design may be illustrated by considering the Fortran realization in which arrays are integer-indexed with unity origin. Defining first a tuple, we have:

```
        tuple[integer]
            declare tuple[integer] → integer
            (tuple[integer] ← integer) → tuple
            newtuple(integer) → tuple
            size(tuple) → integer
            for all t∈tuple and i,j,k∈integer let
            (t[m] ← j)[m] = j
            size(newtuple(i)) = i
    k∈1 .. i => newtuple(i)[k] = 0
    k∉1 .. size(t) => (t[k] = undefined)∧((t[k] ← i) = undefined)
        end
```

Then we build the array with the use of the tuple. (Note the design hierarchy.) Now we have:

```
    Array[item]
        declare array[tuple] → item
        (array[tuple] ← item) → array
        newarray(tuple) → array
        rank(array) → tuple
        for all a∈array and t∈tuple and i∈item and I = (1,1,1...)
        (a[t] ← x)[t] = x
        rank(newarray(t)) = t
    u∈I .. t  =>  newarray(t)[u] = 0
    u∉I .. rank(a)  =>  (a[u] = undefined)∧((a[u] ← x) = undefined)
        end
```

The reader would be correct in observing that this is a lot of machinery for dealing with the familiar concept of arrays. Indeed, the cumbersomeness of the axioms does tend to discourage formal reasoning. However, as the methodology develops, some of the axioms will be taken without restatement just as the axioms of number theory are not restated whenever numbers are used.

5.8 AN EXAMPLE OF PROGRAM VERIFICATION

The purpose of this section is to illustrate in detail the utility of the reasoning processes developed earlier. The example of the "reverse" of a sequence will be used again. The refinement process has already been discussed. Now, suppose we are to verify that the final state of computation meets the condition

$$R: \quad A_j = B_i \, \forall i \in 1 \, .. \, N \text{ and } j = N + 1 - i$$

where A and B are initially identical and the sequence A is reversed by the program. Restating the initial condition, we have:

$$P: \quad A_i = B_i \, \forall i \in 1 \, .. \, N \text{ and integer(I) and integer(N) and } N \geq 0$$

Thus, the initial state of computation is such that I and N are integers. Note that N must be nonnegative (see Figure 5–10).

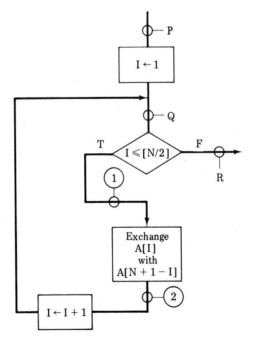

Figure 5–10.   Flow Chart for Reverse of a Sequence.

Utilizing the rule of thumb prescribed for iterations, the loop invariant should express some partial completion of the reversal

$$Q: \quad r[I] \text{ and } s[I]$$

where

$$r[I]: \quad A_i = B_{N+1-i} \text{ and } A_{N+1-i} = B_i \, \forall i \in 1 \ldots I-1$$

$$r[1]: \text{true}$$

$$s[I] = A_i = B_i \, \forall i \in I \ldots N+1-I$$

$$s[\ \lfloor N/2 \rfloor + 1] = \text{true}$$

Here $r[I]$ describes the completed part, and $s[I]$ describes the incomplete part.

To confirm that Q is true the first time, the weakest precondition to the initial assignment is derived from Q. Thus:

$$Q_{I-1}: \quad r[1] \text{ and } s[1]$$

It is easy to see that

$$P \Rightarrow Q_{I-1}: \quad A_i = B_i \, \forall i \in 1 \ldots N$$

Now to show that

$$Q \text{ and } I = \lfloor N/2 \rfloor + 1 \Rightarrow R$$

we note that

$$Q \text{ and } I = \lfloor N/2 \rfloor + 1 \Rightarrow r[\ \lfloor N/2 \rfloor \ ^+1]$$

$$r[[N/2]+1]: \quad A_i = B_{N+1-i} \text{ and } A_{N+1-i} = B_i A i = 1 \ldots [N/2]$$

which is equivalent to R. Thus the desired outcome is assured if Q can be shown to be invariant.

Since the "exchange ... with" segment has already been designed and verified, those results will be used directly:

①: $\quad A[I] = B[I] \wedge A[N+1-I] = B[N+1-I]$

②: $\quad A[I] = B[N+1-I] \wedge A[N+1-I] = B[I]$

For purposes of this computation, the precondition is strengthened to

①': $\quad$ ① $\wedge s[I+1] \wedge r[I]$

Then by enumeration it can be shown that

$$r[I] \wedge s[I] \wedge I \leq \lfloor N/2 \rfloor \Rightarrow ①'$$

Since the "exchange ... with" is "pure" with respect to variables in s[I+1] and r[I], at ② we have

$$\text{②} \quad \Lambda r[I+1] \Lambda s[I] \Rightarrow r[I+1] \text{ and } s[I+1]$$

This is precisely the weakest precondition obtained from

$$Q_{I \leftarrow I+1}$$

Thus Q is invariant.

In order to prove termination, we map the variable, I, onto a well-founded set by

$$t = \lfloor N/2 \rfloor + 1 - I$$

The initial value is

$$t_0 = \lfloor N/2 \rfloor$$

which is greater than or equal to zero since $N \geq 0$. The loop stops whenever $t = 0$. Since I is incremented, t decreases in each iteration. Therefore, termination is assured.

This verification assumed that the computation of $\lfloor N/2 \rfloor$ was correct. It is now left as an exercise to complete the proof by verifying the "floor" operation

The process of verification is perhaps of more interest than the result itself. It involves postulating states before and after the computation by asserting P and R. A loop invariant is constructed by relaxing the completion condition in R. The rules of the calculus of programs are then used to prove that Q is invariant. A well-founded set is constructed in terms of the program state vector, and termination is proven on the basis of transitions within that set.

5.9 PROGRAM CORRECTNESS

Up to this point the discussion of programming methodology has been directed toward "reasoning about programs" as a general concern. The processes of construction and refinement have been oriented toward creating programs that facilitate reasoning of any sort. Examples of formal verification and formal proof of termination have been used to illustrate the reasoning.

Viewed from a broader context, programming methodology, like the rest of software technology, is motivated by correctness and verification concerns. We would like to be able to present convincing arguments, if not proofs, that the program meets its specifications. It has been shown in the case of reasoning about arrays that even very simple structures may require intricate and cumbersome reasoning processes. Thus, the time and effort spent in reasoning may exceed by far the time and effort needed in refinement and construction.

The time and effort devoted to reasoning could be easily justified if the reasoning itself was assuredly correct and reliable. Herein lies the most serious residual problem in programming methodology. It is best defined by considering the distinction between correctness and verification:

> *Correctness:* A program is correct if it performs the intended function.
>
> *Verification:* A program is verified if it performs according to its stated specifications.

The missing link between correctness and verification is the question of whether the *stated specifications* capture the *intended function*. This issue goes back to software design and modularization as the source of the problem. Nonetheless, it is worth noting from experience that program specifications often exist at the limits of human understanding and manageability. Specifications are often more intricate, and thus more error-prone, than the program text that is to be verified. Programmers should not be lured into claiming correctness of a program based on a verification argument. The commitment of time and effort to a verification argument must be tempered by the realization that specifications may need as much or more attention than the verification proof. This deficiency in the methodology is well recognized now and is receiving considerable attention, most notably in the development of formal *design* verification technologies (RL77).

Example 5-1   A Search Algorithm

This example will illustrate the verification of an algorithm to count the occurrences of object, n, in a sequence, x. The flow chart for this algorithm is shown in Figure 5-11.

In the flow chart (Figure 5-11), y is used to count the number of occurrences in the sequence of length $L = |x|$. To verify any algorithm that involves a looping structure requires four steps:

1. Find a suitable loop invariant, Q.
2. Find a well-founded set, WFS.
3. Prove that $P \Rightarrow Q$.
4. Prove that $Q \land \lnot B \Rightarrow R$.

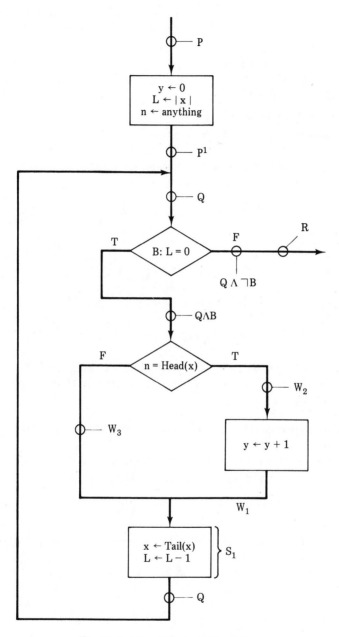

Figure 5-11. A Search Algorithm.

In our example we have two program schemata. The loop part has already been noted. The imbedded conditional part involves five steps:

1. $W_1 \Rightarrow WP(S^1, Q)$.
2. $W_3 \Rightarrow W_1$.
3. $W_2 \Rightarrow WP(y \leftarrow y+1, W_1)$.
4. $(Q \wedge B) \wedge (n = \text{Head}(x)) \Rightarrow W_2$.
5. $(Q \wedge B) \wedge (n \neq \text{Head}(x)) \Rightarrow W_3$.

In the first step of our verification, we must define the precondition, P. Thus:

$$P:\ |\,x\,|\ \text{is defined}$$

This yields a P':

$$P':\ (Y = o) \wedge (L = |\,x\,|) \wedge (|\,x\,|\ \text{is defined})$$

We then must define the postcondition, R.

$$R:\ (Y \cdot N(n \cdot \text{Head}(\text{Tail}^i(x))\ \text{for}\ i \leftarrow (0 \ldots |\,x\,| - 1)))$$

(*Note:* The symbol "N" denotes "number of occurrences of.")

Given the pre- and postconditions, we can now define our loop invariant as follows:

$$Q:\ [y \cdot N(n \cdot \text{Head}(\text{Tail}^i(x)))\ \text{for}\ i \leftarrow (0 \ldots |\,x\,| - L - 1)]$$

Our next step is to prove $Q \wedge \neg B$ implies R. This can be done by substituting $L = 0$ into our loop invariant, Q. This results in R; thus,

$$Q \wedge \neg B \Rightarrow R\ \text{QED}$$

The next step is to prove that P' implies Q. Again this is done by substituting P' into Q.

To prove termination of the loop, our WFS is the length of the buffer, L. Thus:

$$\text{WFS:}\ L = |\,x\,|$$

This completes the first part of our verification proof.

The second part of the proof encounters some difficulty due to the number of occurrences of the operator, N. A mathematical construct to represent this is not available.

At this point is is easier to reevaluate our algorithm than coerce the verification. This is a major advantage of the overall software design methodology, especially in the area of large software packages. The reevaluation will usually point the designer to a better solution to the problem.

In our problem this led to the realization that we are dealing with a boolean function. This eliminates our earlier problem and also reduces the amount of coding. The flow chart is as shown in Figure 5–12. The verification of this algorithm (Figure 5–12) will involve only the four steps required to verify a loop structure. Our loop invariant, Q, is as follows:

$$Q: (y = \sum_{i=1}^{|x_0| - 1 - |x|} int(Head(Tail^i (x_0) = n)))$$

$$B: |x| = 0$$

$$Q \wedge \neg B \Rightarrow R \text{ by inspection QED}$$

$$WFS = |x|$$

$$P \Rightarrow Q \text{ by inspection QED}$$

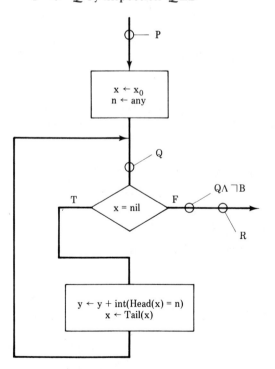

Figure 5–12.   A Simplified Search Algorithm.

Example 5–2   *Verification of Queue Management Operations*

This exercise involves the design and verification of the queue_up and un_queue operations to be applied to a first-in: first-out (by priority) queue. This is typical of queue management operations that arise in multitask systems such as Ada. We will represent the queue as a sequence of pairs:

$$((object, priority) \ldots)$$

The variable, next_space, will represent the next available space in the queue, and max_size will be the maximum numbers of pairs allowed.

The problem will be addressed as though the design had just emerged from the construction of an Ada package:

```
package QUEUE_MGR is
    type QUEUE_PAIR is record
        OBJECT:   any_type;
        PRIORITY:   integer;
    end QUEUE_PAIR;
        procedure QUEUE_UP (P: queue_pair);
        function UN_QUEUE return queue_pair
    end QUEUE_MGR;
```

The problem is to design and verify the package body. We would expect the package body to have the general structure as shown below:

```
package body QUEUE_MGR is
    exception QUEUE_EMPTY, QUEUE_FULL;
    MAX_SIZE: integer: =  256
    NEXT_SPACE: integer: =  0
    QUEUE: array [0..Max_size − 1] of queue pair.
    procedure QUEUE_UP (P: queue_pair)
```
} to be designed

```
function UN_QUEUE return queue_pair
```
} to be designed

exceptions
    When queue_empty $\Rightarrow$ to be designed
    When queue_full $\Rightarrow$ to be designed
end QUEUE_MGR;

The operations, QUEUE_UP and UN_QUEUE, will be required to maintain the priority ordering (PO) and first-in: first-out property (FIFO).

PO: queue[i].priority $\geq$ queue[j].priority $\vee$ i $<$ j

FIFO: arrival time (queue[i]) $\leq$ arrival time (queue[j]) $\vee$ i $<$ j

and queue priority [i] = queue, priority [j]

It will be useful to create two utility programs and abstract their properties in subsequent reasoning. These will be the precessing routines: TAKE_OUT_FIRST and MOVE_UP_AT(J), as shown below:

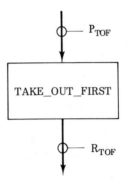

where P_{TOF} is

$$PO \wedge FIFO \wedge (next\_space > 0)$$
$$\wedge (next\_space < max\_size - 1)$$
$$\wedge (next\_space = next\_space')$$
$$\wedge (queue = queue')$$

and R_{TOF} is

$$PO \wedge FIFO \wedge (next\_space = next\_space' - 1)$$
$$\wedge queue[i] = queue' [i+1] \vee i\epsilon(0.. next\_space - 1)$$

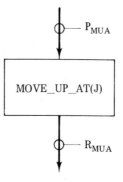

Likewise P_{MUA} is

> PO $\wedge$ FIFO $\wedge$ (next_space $>$ 0)
>
> $\wedge$ (next_space $<$ max_size -2) $\wedge$ (next_space $=$ next_space$'$)
>
> $\wedge$ (J $\geq$ 0) $\wedge$ (J $<$ next_space)
>
> $\wedge$ (queue $=$ queue$'$)

and R_{MUA} is

> PO $\wedge$ FIFO $\wedge$ (next_space $=$ next_space$'$ $+1$)
>
> $\wedge$ queue[i] $=$ queue$'$[i$-$1] $\forall$ iϵ (J$+1$..next_space -1)
>
> $\wedge$ queue[i] $=$ queue$'$[i] $\forall$ iϵ (O..J)

   The QUEUE_UP routine also needs a searching process to locate the spot, J, into which to insert the new pair, as shown here.

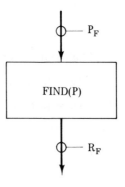

Thus, P_F is

$$PO \wedge FIFO$$

and R_F is

$$PO \land FIFO \land ((J = \text{next\_space}) \text{ or}$$

$$\text{queue[J].Priority} < \text{P.Priority})$$

$$\land ((J = 0 \text{ or}$$

$$\text{queue[J} - 1].\text{Priority} \geq \text{P.Priority})$$

From these abstractions, one can construct the QUEUE_UP routine as shown in Figure 5-13(a) and the UN_QUEUE as shown in Figure 5-13(b).

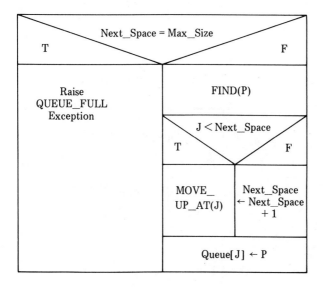

(A)

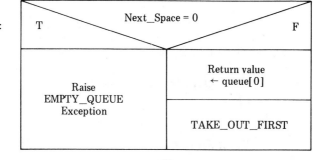

(B)

Figure 5-13   (a) The Queue-Up Module.   (b) The Unqueue Module.

The pre- and postconditions are

where P_{Q_UP} is

$$PO \wedge FIFO \ (P \text{ is a queue pair})$$

and R_{Q_UP} is

$$PO \wedge FIFO \ (P \ \epsilon \text{ queue})$$

or queue was full. Also P_{UN_Q} is

$$PO \wedge FIFO \wedge (Queue = queue')$$

and R_{UN_Q} is

$$PO \wedge FIFO \wedge (\text{return value} = queue'[0])$$

or queue was empty.

It is apparent from the proposed structure that the following proofs must be completed:

1. $P_{Q\_UP} \wedge (Next\_Space = Max\_Size) \Rightarrow R_{Q\_UP}$

   and

   $P_{Q\_UP} \Rightarrow P_F$

2. $R_F \wedge (J < Next\_Space) \Rightarrow P_{MUA}$

   and

   $R_F \wedge (J \geq Next\_Space) \Rightarrow WP(S_1; S_2, R_{QUP})$

3. $R_{MUA} \Rightarrow WP(S_2; R_{Q\_UP})$

Where S_1 is Next_Space ← Next_Space + 1, we have

S_2 is queue[J] ← P

Likewise for the UNQUEUE routine:

1. $P_{UN\_Q} \wedge (Next\_Space = 0) \Rightarrow R_{UN\_Q}$

   and

   $P_{UN\_Q} \wedge (Next\_Space = 0) \Rightarrow WP(S_3, P_{TOF})$

2. $R_{TOF} \Rightarrow R_{UN\_Q}$

where S_3 is return value ← queue[0].

The verification has now been reduced to the five above proofs and the separate verification of the elementary steps TAKE_OUT_ FIRST, MOVE_UP_AT (J), and FIND(P). Since no recovery is possible in the case of the "queue full" exception, the package would be designed to produce an error message. The "queue empty" exception could be propagated and handled within the UN_QUEUE function, thus appearing as:

When queue_empty ⇒ return value.object ← Nil;

return value.Priority ← 0;

The detailed verifications of TAKE_OUT_FIRST, MOVE_UP_ AT(J), and FIND(P) would follow patterns very similar to those of the previous exercise and the example discussed in Section 5.8. It should be noted that a key to the development illustrated has been the identification of the properties PO and FIFO, which are subsequently enforced at every stage of the development. They become natural candidates for components of the loop invariants that will be needed in the subordinate routines. However, the PO and FIFO conditions have become so universal in their scope that they may also be dropped from subsequent reasoning provided it can be guaranteed that no more elementary step would lead to violation of the conditions. For instance, during precession, the operations:

$$queue[i] \leftarrow queue [i+1]$$

and

$$queue[i] \leftarrow queue [i-1]$$

would not cause a violation. (*Note:* The PO and FIFO predicates include equality relations.) Likewise, since FIND(P) leaves the queue unchanged, it also cannot lead to a violation. That leaves only the question of insertion within the QUEUE_UP routine. The validity of PO is guaranteed by the postcondition on FIND(P). The FIFO condition is guaranteed by the fact that P has not yet "arrived" upon invocations of the QUEUE_UP routine.

In consideration of the above observations, the completion of the reasoning will be illustrated by constructively verifying the FIND(P), routine, noting

P_F is True

R_F is $((J = next\_space)$ or $queue[J].Priority < P.Priority)$

$\Lambda((J = 0)$ or $queue[J-1].Priority \geq P.Priority)$

The postcondition is reformulated as

$$R_F \text{ is } Q \Lambda \daleth B$$

where B is

$((J - next\_space)$ and $queue[J].Priority \geq P.Priority)$

and Q is

$(J = 0)$ or $queue[J-1].Priority \geq P.Priority)$

It is convenient to introduce a new state variable, FOUND, such that

$$B \text{ is } (J = \text{Next\_Space}) \text{ and FOUND}$$

$$Q \text{ is } (J = 0) \text{ or queue}[J - 1].\text{Priority} \geq P.\text{Priority}$$

$$\wedge \text{ FOUND } \Rightarrow \text{ queue}[J].\text{Priority} < P.\text{Priority}$$

The predicate, Q, is now a candidate for the loop invariant in Figure 5-14. Here B′ is queue[J − 1].Priority ≥ P.Priority.

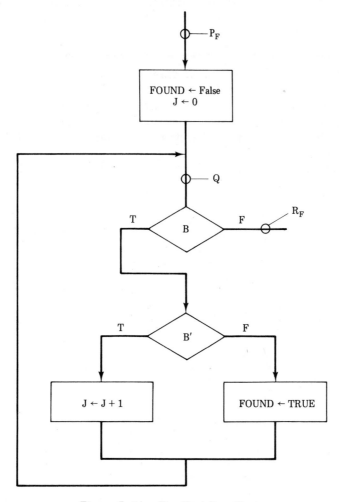

Figure 5-14. The Find Algorithm.

The verification is completed by showing that

1. $Q \land B \land B' \Rightarrow WP(J \leftarrow J + 1, Q)$.

2. $Q \land B \land B' \Rightarrow WP(FOUND \leftarrow True, Q)$.

3. $(Next\_Space - J) \times Integer(Found)$ is a suitable well-founded set.

4. $((J = 0) \land FOUND) \Rightarrow Q$.

The remaining details of the proofs are left as an exercise. The intent of this example has been to show the influence of the design methodology (i.e., Ada) on the verification process, and also to illustrate the pervasiveness of the construction of computational invariants such as PO and FIFO.

Example 5-3 *A Direct Application of Inductive Reasoning*

The purpose of this exercise is to illustrate the role of inductive reasoning in the verification of specific program designs. Inductive logic has already been employed extensively to show the relationship between loop invariants and weakest preconditions.

The familiar example of the reversal of a data sequence may be cast in a recursive form:

> proc Rev (x,y);
>
> > if x is Nil then y
> >
> > > else Rev (Tail(x), cons(Head(x),y))

where Lisp notation is utilized in the cons, Head, and Tail operations. In the simplest case, the function would be invoked by

> Rev(A,Nil)

and the result would be the reversal of A. In the usual flow-chart form, the program is as shown in Figure 5-15. We will denote the reversal as x^R, and state the verification conditions as

$$P \text{ is } (Y = Nil) \land (X \text{ is a list})$$
$$R \text{ is } (Val = X^R)$$

and note the fundamental properties:

$$X^R = Append (Tail(X)^R, Cons(Head(X),Nil))$$
$$Nil^R = Nil$$

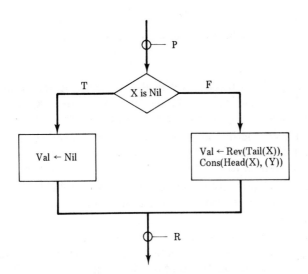

Figure 5-15.   A Recursive Reverse Algorithm.

That is, the reversal can be formed by moving the head to the right end and attaching the reversal of the tail to the left.

To show that any state in P, when followed by the indicated computation, leaves the state in R, one begins with the base case:

Base case: X is Nil

For this case it is sufficient to show that

$$P \wedge (X \text{ is Nil}) \implies WP(Val \leftarrow Nil, R)$$

which is equivalent to

$$P \wedge (X \text{ is Nil}) \implies Nil = X^R$$

which is true from the second fundamental property of X^R.

For the inductive part, suppose that we assume that the program is correct for the tail of X. That is,

$$Rev(Tail(X), Z) = Append(Tail(X)^R, Z) \text{ for all } Z$$

Then for the particular case of Z = Cons(Head(X), Nil), we have

$$Append(Tail(X)^R, cons(Head(X), Nil)) = X^R$$

The inductive assumption was strengthened to apply to the tail of X and all Z in order to argue that it also applies to X.

ADDITIONAL EXERCISES

1. Develop a constructive verification of a string match algorithm suitable for use in Snobol. Note points at which the verification methodology may be more error-prone than the implementation.
2. Extend the methodology of program verification to:
   (a) Multiple tasks synchronized by semaphores.
   (b) Ada rendezvous (see LG81, pp. 281–302).
3. Suggest a verification methodology that would deal effectively with bounds on error propagation in computations with real numbers.
4. At least a part of the methodology developed in this chapter encouraged a process of abstraction away from irrelevant detail. Suggest some pathological situations wherein these same details may come back to haunt a software project during systems integration (e.g., failure to consider a time budget may make the system violate real-time constraints).

REFERENCES

(BM75)   Basu, S. K., and J. Misra, "Proving Loop Programs," *Transactions of Software Engineering*, vol. SE-1 (1975).

(BJ66)   Bohm, C., and G. Jacopini, "Flow Diagrams, Turing Machines and Languages With Only Two Formation Rules," *Communications of the ACM*, vol. 19 (1966).

(Br75)   Brooks, F. P., *The Mythical Man-Month*. Reading, Mass.: Addison-Wesley Publishing Co., Inc., 1975.

(Bu69)   Burstall, R. M., "Proving Properties of Programs by Structural Induction," *The Computer Journal*, vol. 12 (1969).

(DDH72)   Dahl, O. J., E. W. Dijkstra, and C. A. R. Hoare, *Structured Programming*. New York: Academic Press, Inc., 1972.

(Di68)   Dijkstra, E. W., "Go To Statement Considered Harmful," *Communications of the ACM*, vol. 11 (1968).

(Di76)   Dijkstra, E. W., *A Discipline of Programming*. Englewood Cliffs, N.J.: Prentice-Hall, Inc., 1976.

(GHM78)   Gutlag, J. V., E. Horowitz, and D. R. Musser, "The Design of Data Type Specifications," *Current Trends in Programming Methodology*, vol. IV (1978).

(LG81)   Levin, G. M., and D. Gries, "A Proof Technique for Communicating Sequential Processes," *Acta Informatica*, vol. 15 (1981).

(Mi75)   Mills, H. D., "The New Math of Computer Programming," *Communications of the ACM*, vol. 18 (1975).

(RL77)   Robinson, L., and K. N. Levitt, "Proof Techniques for Hierarchically Structured Programs," *Current Trends in Programming Methodology*, vol. II. Englewood Cliffs, N.J.: Prentice-Hall, Inc., 1977.

(St78)   Standish, T. A., "Data Structures: An Axiomatic Approach," *Current Trends in Programming Methodology*, vol. IV. Englewood Cliffs, N.J.: Prentice-Hall, Inc., 1978.

(Wi73)   Wirth, N., *Systematic Programming*. Englewood Cliffs, N.J.: Prentice-Hall, Inc., 1973.

(Ye77)   Yeh, R. T., "Verification of Programs by Predicate Transformation," *Current Trends in Programming Methodology*, vol. II. Englewood Cliffs, N.J.: Prentice-Hall, Inc., 1977.

Case Studies

6

6.1 A RELATIONAL DATA BASE

The case study presented here is the product of several student projects intended to design and implement a relational data base. The task was chosen because it represents a problem that in spite of some implementations is as yet unsolved, and thus there is a real challenge in establishing some integrity for the software. The relational data base is a significant departure from earlier realizations of large-scale bases in that the software is obliged to create a powerful, yet convenient, user-oriented model of the data. Earlier models of data base systems (i.e., hierarchical and network systems) imposed a greater burden on the user to adopt and understand the implementation model of the data.

This chapter will present the results of specification and design of the relational data base. As the discussion approaches final implementation, the presentation will be more selective, and thus the material should be viewed as illustrative only. The magnitude of the whole task is approximated only by extrapolating the illustrations over the entire design.

In the interest of making this presentation self-contained for the reader who might be unfamiliar with data base technology, the fundamentals of relational data bases will be presented. The reader is referred to several excellent texts for more thorough treatments of the ideas (Da76), (TL77).

For a relational data base, the user views the data as a realization of the mathematical notion of a *relation*. A relation is a set of n-tuples where the set is usually specified by a property that each of the n-tuples possesses. The relation is often named by that property, such as the "greater than" relation. In data bases, we are usually concerned with finite relations such as the "situated in" relation. For example:

$$\text{situated in} \equiv \{(\text{New York, U.S.}), (\text{Cairo, Egypt}),$$

$$(\text{London, U.K.}), \dots \}$$

Such a relation is conveniently viewed as a table:

situated in:

CITY	COUNTRY
New York	U. S.
Cairo	Egypt
London	U. K.

The relation may have any number of columns (domains) and rows (elements), but since it is a set, there may not be repeated elements. There is a presumption of homogeneity within the domains, and thus the type such as "CITY" may be dissociated from each element individually.

A relational data base software system implements useful accesses and manipulations of relations. In the interest of integrity, the results of the operations on relations are to be viewed as relations. For example, given the above "situated in" relation, the response to the query "What city is in Egypt?" would be:

situated in Egypt:

CITY
CAIRO

The language utilized by the user of a relational data base may take many forms. A "relational calculus" has been proposed as a user language in an attempt to remove all "proceduralness" from the user view of data manipulations. The underlying primitive operations on the data are conveniently realized by a "relational algebra," which tends to hide proceduralness within relations but does not hide the sequence of intermediate relations that may be required to get a desired result.

This discussion of the user language and underlying operations immediately begins to suggest a modularization of the software, but lest the excitement of immediate creativity carry us away, it will pay to pause and consider the requirements of the software.

6.1.1 Requirements Specification

The purpose of this section is to illustrate the results of requirements specification for the relational data base system. One might first attempt to state some general principles to be adhered to in the software:

GENERAL PRINCIPLES

The software proposed here is intended to provide the means of creating, updating, and accessing large aggregates of data. The software should not dictate the organization of the data as viewed by the user. In assessing design trade-offs, it should be kept in mind that the software will be employed by a variety of organizations (i.e., in a variety of applications) where in each application the data is acquired from a variety of sources and is accessed by a variety of users.

This statement of principles is an attempt to capture the important considerations from the buyer's point of view. No mention is made of relations, languages, or machines. Note some terms have already been introduced that need clarification.

DEFINITION OF TERMS

1. *Large aggregates of data:* The notion of largeness here is closely tied to the variety of sources and users. It is important that the software not impose arbitrary constraints on the size of the data base.
2. *Intended:* Indicates a goal that must be met by the software.
3. *Should:* Indicates a highly desirable feature of the software.

The state of the art in data base technology is brought into the general design criteria.

GENERAL DESIGN CRITERIA

The data base software should achieve the highest possible level of generality in the user's point of view. In this consideration, the relational data base model is proposed as the least general but acceptable level of realization. Where the user does not have explicit control of sequencing of data accesses (i.e., due to a nonprocedural language), the software should optimize the sequence of accesses. The data base software should support a security system that conforms to legal standards and allows distinctions between maintainers (data base administrators) and users with query rights only.

This part of the requirements specification raises specific technical issues that are to be considered in the design such as generality, optimization, and security. By dealing with them in general terms they become somewhat unquantifiable goals. In one case, the relational data base is proposed as a minimally acceptable model.

Specific requirements for the software may be dealt with in a more detailed statement as noted in the following page.

SPECIFIC REQUIREMENTS

1. *User language:* The user language facility will provide as a minimum a single scope aggregate naming facility and means of composing arbitrary functions from the relational algebra. Highly desirable facilities would include explicit blocking of scopes, iterative and conditional controls, and specification of functions in the relational calculus.

2. *The interpreter:* The underlying software must constitute a full realization of the operations of the relational algebra.

3. *Security:* All user interfaces will be secured by password authentication. All interfaces with other data base systems will be secured by encryption. Protection against data inferences will be maintained by the data base administrator. The user maintains private rights to any relation created or derived unless that relation is explicitly made available to another user. Relinquishing private rights applies to only one relation and one new user at a time. Thus there are no implicit rights.

6.1.2 *Software Design*

The data base software proposed here represents an attempt to achieve the stated requirements and to maintain a high level of integrity in the design. The key to the integrity will be in the structure of a storage model that is sympathetic to the relational abstraction and in the imposition of severe limits on the number of data types employed.

THE DESIGN PHILOSOPHY

In the interest of integrity, simplicity of design, and maintainability, the *relation* (as a data abstraction) will be used throughout as the primary composite data structure. The software may be viewed as a "relation machine" superimposed on the host.

AN ANALOGOUS DESIGN

Just as great cathedrals are inspired by prior architectural triumphs, so this software is inspired by the Lisp programming system. Since relations are sets rather than n-tuples as in lists, the logical interpretation is in terms of nondeterminant computation analogues to guarded commands.

AN OVERALL DESIGN

The overall structure may be viewed as a hierarchy of modules organized as shown in Figure 6-1.

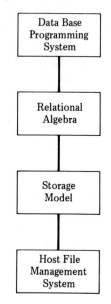

Figure 6-1.   Overall Design of a Relational Data Base System.

Since there is more to be specified than the hierarchy, the module specifications may be detailed through the medium proposed in Chapter 4; see Figure 6-2(a)-(e).

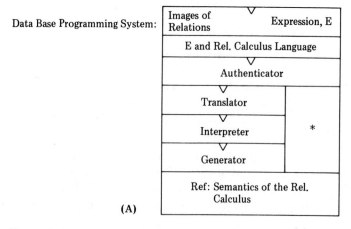

Figure 6-2.   (a) Overall Design of a Data Base System. *(Continued)*

Interpreter:

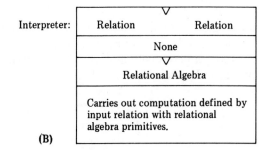

(B)

Translator:

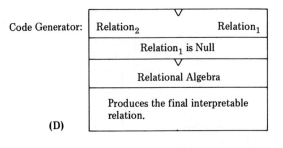

(C)

Code Generator:

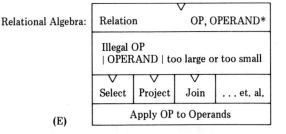

(D)

Relational Algebra:

Relation	OP, OPERAND*
Illegal OP	OPERAND	too large or too small	
Select	Project	Join	... et. al.
Apply OP to Operands	

(E)

Figure 6-2.   (b) The Interpreter Module.   (c) The Translator Module.   (d) The Code Generator Module.   (e) The Relational Algebra Module.

At this point, the hierarchy of the design has been specified to the level shown in Figure 6-3. Although the design is incomplete, the process is clearly manageable. The refinement of detail involves continuing the decomposition, and, equally importantly, reworking the specifications (exceptions and effects) to make them more precise.

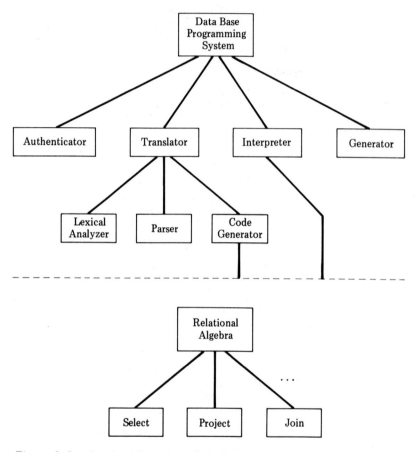

Figure 6-3.   Another View of the Overall Design of the Data Base System.

6.1.3 *Program Design*

The purpose of this section is to carry one of the modules developed in the previous section through the programming and verification process. *Selection,* which is one of the primitive operations of the relational algebra, will be programmed and verified. As a first step, the Select module will be partially specified (see Figure 6-4).

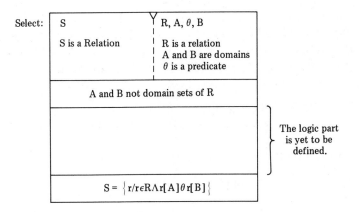

Figure 6-4. The Select Module.

The notation r[A] is borrowed from the mathematical treatment of the relational algebra. If

$$A = (D_1, D_2, \ldots, D_k)$$

then r[A] is the tuple formed by

$$(r[D_1], r[D_2], \ldots, r[D_k])$$

The $r[D_i]$ are components of the tuple r.

The logic part is constructed from the module specifications by using the "exceptions" and "effects" part as a basis for formulating pre-and postconditions on the program. Since each element of the starting relation must be examined, an iterative process can be expected. The program would be constructed to hold the following invariant at some point in the iteration:

$$Q: (\forall t \epsilon S)(t \epsilon R_0 \wedge t \not\epsilon R \wedge t[A] \theta t[B]) \wedge (\forall u \epsilon R_0 - S - R)(\neg u[A] \theta u[B])$$

When constructed as a WHILE. . DO, the program predicate would be

$$TEST: \ R \neq NULL$$

The derived postcondition would then be

$$Q \wedge \neg TEST$$

The first step of the verification would be to show that

$$Q \wedge \neg TEST \ \Rightarrow \ S = \{r \mid r \epsilon R \vee r[A] \theta r[B]\}$$

Assuming such a proof can be completed, the remainder of the program would be formulated to keep Q invariant. The module specifications, together with an assertion that S is initially null, are sufficient to assure Q upon entering the iteration. The body of the iteration may take the form

$$r,R: = next(R)$$
$$\text{if } Apply(\theta,r[A],r[B]) \text{ then } S: = S \cup r$$

The verification proceeds by proving that

$$Q \Lambda B \;\Rightarrow\; WP(body,Q)$$

Termination would be assured by formulating a well-founded set in terms of the program state vector. A suitable well-founded set would be the size of R:

$$t = |R|$$

which can be shown to decrease if "next" is properly designed, and termination occurs when $t = 0$.

At this stage of design, several refinements have been clearly identified. These include next, Apply, [ ], and union ($\cup$). The process illustrated above would continue as necessary to a convenient set of primitive operations.

The design and logical specification are ultimately realized in a program text. In the case of the Select module, the text may take the following form (*Note:* { } will be used to indicate commentary):

```
procedure Select(S,R,A,θ,B)
    {S is the value returned; a relation;
    R is the starting relation;
    A and B are domain sets of R;
    θ is a predicate}
    S: = NULL
    WHILE {(∀tεS)(tεR₀Λt∉RΛt[A]θt[B])Λ(∀uεR₀ − S − R)(∀u[A]-
θu[B])}
        R ≠ NULL  DO
                    r,R: = NEXT(R)
                    if Apply (θ,r[A],r[B])
                        then S: = S∪r
                    fi
                    OD
    {S = {r|rεRΛr[A]θr[B]}}
    end
```

At this point a prototype program has been designed, and a relevant logical commentary has been extracted from the module specifications. There are some verification steps yet to be fully detailed. As noted above, the following remains to be proven:

$$Q \wedge \neg TEST \implies S = \{r \mid r\epsilon R \wedge r[A]\theta r[B]\}$$
$$Q \wedge TEST \implies WP(body, Q)$$
$$\mid B \mid \text{ decreasing in every iteration}$$

The proofs are straightforward using the methodology of Chapter 5. This example of program design serves to illustrate the interactions between the verification and program construction processes.

6.2 COMPILER DESIGN

The study of compiler design offers an opportunity to examine what is now a thoroughly developed and classic case of software design. This case has survived as an intriguing problem throughout the decades of development of software engineering. The understanding of compiler design has matured to a point that it is now standard practice to automate much of the implementation of compilers.

6.2.1 Requirements Statements for a Compiler

The requirements for compilers are naturally stated in terms of a language design. Since our understanding of the formal structures of language has developed to the point of allowing mathematical descriptions of syntax, semantics, and semantically invariant transformations (i.e., optimization), this case is unusual in that mathematical notation can be brought to bear on the requirements statements. Consider as an example the language description given below that is an example of a syntax-directed translation. Each syntactic rule is followed by the specification of its corresponding interpretable code. The purpose of the compiler is to accept programs described by the syntax and to produce code described by the semantics.

Example of a Syntax-Directed Translation

Program:: = ikw infix_exp {mkw infix_exp} [ekw] $\Rightarrow$ sm_kwe
           | infix_exp $\Rightarrow$ sm_infix_exp

Infix_exp:: = fn_form $\Rightarrow$ SM_FF
             | fn_form OP infix_exp $\Rightarrow$ sm_infix_exp
             | (Program) $\Rightarrow$ SM_P

fn_form:: =   id ⇒ ID

|fn_form_op ([Program {, Program}]) ⇒ sm_fn_form

|literal ⇒ LITERAL

fn_form_op:: =   fn_form

Note: The syntactic notation is the same as that employed by the Ada designers (i.e., see Appendix B). The " = >" indicates reference to the corresponding semantic structure.)

Although the choice of semantic structure is usually prescribed only informally in language design, the essential features may be elaborated in a language such as DIANA (GW81).

<u>Example of a Semantic Definition</u>

SM_PROGRAM:: =   sm_kwe

| SM_INFIX_EXP

SM_INFIX_EXP:: =   SM_FN_FORM

| sm_infix_exp

| SM_PROGRAM

SM_FN_FORM:: =   ID

| sm_fn_form

| LITERAL

SM_FN_FORM_OP:: =   FN_FORM

sm_kwe ⇒   *key words*   : seq_of_KW

operands   : seq_of_SM_INFIX_EXP

sm_infix_exp ⇒   *operator*   : OP

L-operand   : SM_FN_FORM

R-operand   : SM_INFIX_EXP

sm_fn_form ⇒   *operator*   : SM_FN_FORM_OP

arguments   : seq_of_SM_PROGRAM

(*Note:* The symbols "::=" and "=>" take on new significance in the semantic context. The former indicates a set of alternate definitions. The latter indicates a labeled composite structure.)

It is plausible (but not always practical) to pass the SM_ PROGRAM to a computer for execution. Here we attempt what amounts to a mathematical description of the requirements for the compiler. Thus, this case is not a good example of the stated methodology of Chapter 3. It is interesting to note, however, that the less formal requirements statements have been pushed into the language design domain. The IRONMAN example found in Chapter 3 derives from an attempt to state requirements for a lnaguage design as opposed to compiler design.

It is important to note that the syntax and semantics are stated in terms of designed languages: BNF and DIANA, respectively. Descriptions of these languages may be subjected to the same analysis, thus leading to such extended notions as syntax of syntax, semantics of syntax, syntax of semantics, and semantics of semantics. Rather than casual recursion, these observations are the key to "bootstrapping" compilers into existence. The original syntax and semantics are likely to be large, unwieldy, and unstable. The bootstrap languages are small, humanly manageable, and stable. Through the use of bootstrapping techniques, one is able to avoid software design activity that is in any way a function of the size of the language being compiled.

6.2.2 Design of a Compiler

Many of the design features of compilers are a result of a history of numerous attempts at design rather than a conscious design process. The typical design is of the form shown in Figure 6-5. The subordinate components are shown in Figure 6-6(a) and (b). In Figure 6-6(b), the subordinates Predict, Scan, and Complete handle the nonterminals, terminals, and end-of-rule states, respectively, for the syntax processing.

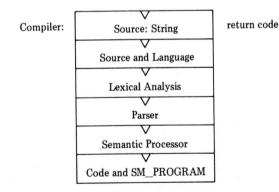

Figure 6-5.   Overall Design of a Compiler.

Lexical Analysis:

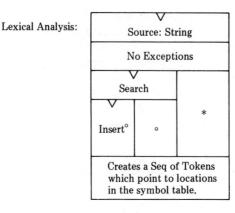

(A)

Parser:

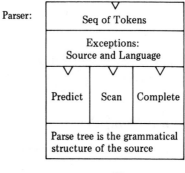

(B)

Figure 6-6.   (a) The Lexical Analysis Module.   (b) The Parser Module.

The semantic processing module is intended to walk through (or equivalently, execute) the parse tree that is produced by the parser module. Each node of the parse tree represents a rule in the syntactic description, and, as such, there is a corresponding semantic object to be created at that node. The subordinate modules reduce to constructors for sm_kwe, sm_infix_exp, and sm_fn_form in the preceding example.

6.2.3 Program Verification

In spite of the precision of the requirements statements and the standardization of the design of compilers, the detailed verification of the major components is still a very challenging process. The problem arises from the fact that the specifications are more intricate and error-prone than the program being created. The mathematical underpinnings are well developed, and when the process is approached in the context of formal language theory, we find extensive machinery at hand to reason about the equivalence between acceptors (parsers) and grammars (syntax). To the program designer, however, the need for a constructive reasoning process is apparent if we examine the logic of the part of the parser that would process the infix_exp of the example language; see Figure 6-7.

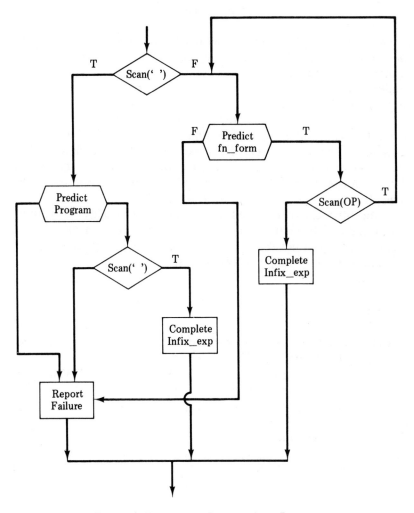

Figure 6-7.   Logical Design of the Parser.

Since the logic shown in Figure 6–7 is a direct derivative of the syntax description, the syntax (i.e., in BNF) may be viewed as a programming language for parsers. (In fact, most descriptions of the syntax of Pascal are given in such a flow-chart type of language.) The point is that syntax design is itself a programming methodology. With suitable bootstrapping facilities, the verification of the logic shown in Figure 6–7 is supplanted by verification that the syntax describes the intended language. That is, Can it be shown that all source strings of the form

$$F(G(Y)) \; (H(Z))$$

are in the language? Or, perhaps, we may wish to verify that all properly parenthesized infixed expressions are legal. One verification process requires some independent descriptor of the language such as a universally understood example—statements such as "All properly ..." or regular expressions (HU79).

As a case study in software technology, the compiler design problem is both illustrative of, and contradictory to, the methodology developed in the first five chapters of this text. The problem tends to support the development of mathematical tools for requirements statements. The modularization of the compiler tends to follow conventional lines. The programming methodology developed in Chapter 5 is subverted by both the intricacies of the specifications and the availability of bootstrapping facilities. The mathematical details remain in the domain of formal language theory. A development of the ultimate verification machinery remains beyond the scope of this discussion.

REFERENCES

(Da76)   Date, C. J., *An Introduction to Data Base Systems*. Reading, Mass.: Addison-Wesley Publishing Co., Inc., 1976.

(GW81)   Goos, G., and W. A. Wulf, DIANA Reference Manual. Washington, D.C.: Department of Defense, 1981.

(HU79)   Hopcroft, J. E., and J. D. Ullman, *Introduction to Automata Theory, Languages, and Computation*. Reading, Mass.: Addison-Wesley Publishing Co., Inc., 1979.

(TL77)   Tsichritzis, D. C., and F. H. Lochovsky, *Data Base Management Systems*. New York: Academic Press, Inc., 1977.

Testing

7

7.1 TRADITIONAL TESTING METHODOLOGY

Software and program testing are important technological concerns that arise naturally from the overall issue of software verification. Regardless of how painstaking the analysis and design have been, there is a still higher level of confidence to be obtained by testing the final product. What is gained from the testing effort is highly dependent on the degree of scientific thinking (i.e., technology) that enters into the design of the test plan.

As with most aspects of software technology, analogies may be found in other technologies that help us to see this new technology in perspective. A distinction is usually made between *component testing* and systems *integration testing.* In the first type of testing, we may find laboratory tests run on samples of concrete or structural components for a bridge. The ideas of sampling and inference from samples become important steps in component testing. The second type of testing, integration testing, usually takes place after implementation and may involve a certain amount of risk taking. For example, there may be a failure in integration testing such as an airplane crash or a nuclear reactor accident, and an investigative panel is then formed to determine the cause of the failure. Corrective designs and improved new designs would be formulated from the results of the investigation.

In software, the analogy to component testing is the testing of an individual module or routine. However, the approach to testing a single component is not the same as found in other technologies. Instead of a multiplicity of objects and a single critical test, we are dealing with a single object, the program, and a multiplicity of tests with little knowledge of which test is critical. Thus the sampling is to be done from a population of *test cases* rather than from a population of like objects. Perhaps the best analogy to this kind of testing is the diagnostic testing of blood samples in a medical application.

Program testing (i.e., component testing in this context) has been an important part of programming methodology from the beginning. However, even the most exacting of programming methods tend to leave errors in the program, errors that are not discovered until the program is executed. We have come to expect a "debugging" phase of program development, and we tend to value sophisticated debugging tools. Traditional approaches to debugging involve attempts to exercise as much of the program as possible without exhaustively examining the entire domain of the program. Experience of several decades of this type of testing indicates that 90 percent of the errors may be found and removed, but the remaining 10 percent are very difficult to remove through the traditional approaches. Since some programs deal with

142

unlimited domains of data, the alternate of exhaustive testing is also out of the question.

Another particularly troublesome aspect of component testing arises when there is no reliable reference for the test result. We may not know the right answer! More likely, we have the program result and another result that may be as error-prone as the program result (i.e., a hand calculation). Thus the testing process may introduce errors rather than remove them.

The state of the art in component testing as described above was evident when the more modern programming methodology began to emerge. It led Dijkstra to observe that testing may prove the existence of errors but not their absence. Programming methodology as described in Chapter 5 has been, in part, motivated by the need for program design techniques that would preclude testing as part of the verification process.

A renewed interest in component testing has emerged with the realization that other verification techniques are also error-prone. Logical assertions about a program are often as intricate as the program itself, and thus the reasoning may begin with fallacious premises. The proof steps are also subject to error. Therefore the current testing techniques are oriented toward exploiting the strengths of both direct reasoning and sampling in the process of verification.

The development of integration testing has tended to follow conventional lines as it has in other technologies. The motivation behind integration testing is to resolve difficulties that may have arisen because the specifications were incomplete. Questions of average and peak time, cost, and resource utilization may be answered through testing. What is known as performance testing and benchmarking would also fall in this category. The important feature is that the software is implemented and, in some sense, is tested in a user environment.

Integration testing of software has a unique feature that arises from what Brooks called the "exceedingly tractable medium" (Br75). Although we have no reason to believe that catastrophic failure may occur, such a belief can lead to denial when it does happen, and thus the post-mortems are likely to be inadequate and uninstructive. The entire technology is in need of a long-range plan for investigating failures and for sharing design conclusions that arise from the investigations.

7.2 A THEORY OF PROGRAM TESTING

The theoretical foundations of program testing have received renewed interest in light of the pitfalls inherent in other methodologies. The theoretical structure that has emerged tends to illuminate some of the important technical issues in testing, but a process-oriented theory remains to be developed.

In the simplest cases, we can presume a program, P, to be a realization of a funcion, f, defined on a domain, D. The program may be an imperfect realization. Thus it is actually a realization of the *program function*, [P]. The program would be considered correct if it terminates and if

$$(\forall d \epsilon D) \quad [P(d)] = f(d)$$

The testing problem may be defined as finding the minimum subset of D on which a test will infer correctness. Thus:

$$\underset{T \leq D}{\text{Min.}} \quad (\forall t \epsilon T) \ [P(t)] = f(t) \Rightarrow (\forall d \epsilon D) [P(d)] = f(d))$$

Therefore T is the minimum subset of the domain that will guarantee correctness over the entire domain. Any such candidate subset of D is called a *test*, and a single element of the test (i.e., $t \epsilon T$) is called a *test case*.

Since the number of candidates for tests is very large (i.e., the power set of D), it is convenient to partition the subsets into equivalence classes and assert some essential properties of the equivalence classes. A test criterion, C(T), might be proposed as a means of narrowing the field of candidate tests. The C(T) would be a predicate defined over all subsets of D. In conventional approaches to testing, an implied criterion might be "all those tests that exercise every logical path."

In the interest of inferring correctness, one might assert some desirable properties of the test criterion. These properties relate to the outcome of the test. Thus a successful test is first defined by

$$\text{SUCCESSFUL (T)} \equiv (\forall t \epsilon T) [P(t)] = f(t)$$

That is, for a successful test, no error is encountered in any test case. The criterion is said to be reliable (Go79), (GG77) if the following is true:

$$\text{Reliable (C)} \equiv (\forall T_1, T_{2c} D) \ (C(T_1) \wedge C(T_2) \Rightarrow$$
$$(\text{SUCCESSFUL } (T_1) \equiv \text{SUCCESSFUL } (T_2))$$

In other words, the tests identified by the criterion are either all successful or they are all unsuccessful. In like manner, the notion of validity of a test criterion is defined by

$$\text{Valid (C)} \equiv (\forall d \epsilon D)(\neg OK(d) \Rightarrow (\exists T \leq D) (C(T) \wedge \neg SUCCESSFUL(T))$$

where

$$OK(d) \equiv [P(d)] = f(d)$$

In other words, if any test fails, then that test must be selectable by the criterion. The criterion does not systematically exclude the unsuccessful tests, but, of course, not every test specified by the criterion will give the same result unless the criterion is also reliable.

The above development leads naturally to the correctness theorem for tests:

CORRECTNESS THEOREM

1. If a test is selected by a test criterion, and
2. If the criterion can be shown to be reliable and valid, and
3. If the test is successful,
   then the program is correct.

Informally, the proof of this theorem follows by assuming the program is not correct. Then, a valid criterion must identify a test that contains the incorrect case. A reliable criterion would then produce tests that all fail. Therefore, the test could not be successful, a contradiction of premise No. 3 above.

As noted in the introductory discussion, this theoretical development tends to focus attention on the important issue of *test criteria*. Given a candidate criterion, one must be able to prove reliability and validity in order to infer correctness.

At this point, the theory of testing presents a serious dilemma. The verification of the test criterion will require an ever-more detailed analysis of error sources and classification. In order to argue validity of a test criterion, one must be able to argue that certain errors are not systematically excluded. This argument requires such careful specification of errors that if these errors were present, they would easily be found and removed before the test was performed. Thus the methodology that might develop around this theory of testing may not be a testing (empirical) methodology.

7.3 SYMBOLIC EXECUTION

As an alternate to the selection of test cases for program verification, it is possible to think of the test case in symbolic terms. Instead of a specific data item being passed through a program, imagine the result of applying the program to a symbolic representation of the data item. The role of the symbol is to provide the universal quantifier in the expression

$$(\forall d \epsilon D)\,[P(d)] = f(d)$$

Thus, the focus of testing is shifted from the selection of (d) to the verification of

$$[P(d)] = f(d)$$

Another verification methodology can now be described in terms of the process:

1. Select a program.
2. Derive the program function, [P]
3. Prove that the program function is the intended function.

Similar to the methodology developed in Chapter 5, a calculus of program functions can be established to deal with Step 2 of this process (LMW79). The first step is heuristic in nature, and the last step may require special mathematical arguments regarding equivalence of functions.

Although a good deal of attention is being given to automating Step 2 of the above process, it will be discussed here in terms of a textual analysis of programs that might be performed by the programmer. In a spirit very similar to the predicate transformers, the program functions for some primitive components will be given, and composition rules will be developed.

In mathematics, we would expect to represent the program function as a set of ordered pairs (X,Y) such that the value of Y is unique given X. The set of ordered pairs may be specified by complete enumeration:

$$\{(X_1,Y_1),(X_2,Y_2) \cdots (X_n,Y_n)\}$$

or more commonly by logical constraints of the form

$$\{(X,Y \mid Q(X,Y)\}$$

where Q is some logical expression on the elements of the pair. For example, consider a program with a state vector (x,y,z), which performs the assignment

$$x: = y$$

Then the program function is

$$[x:=y] \ = \ \{(x,y,z), (u,v,w) \mid u=y, v=y, w=z\}$$

Likewise, a sequence of functions, f and g, produces

$$[f;g] \ = \ \{(X,Y) \mid Y \ = \ g(f(X))\}$$

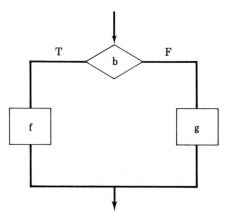

Figure 7-1. The if. . then. . else Form.

The program function for an if. .then. .else of the form shown in Figure 7–1 is as follows:

$$[if \ b \ then \ f \ else \ g] \ = \ \{ \ (X,Y) \mid$$
$$b(X) \ \Rightarrow \ Y \ = \ f(X)$$
$$\Lambda \ \lnot \ b(X) \ \Rightarrow \ Y \ = \ g(X) \}$$

The sequence of functions and the if. .then. .else case are examples of composition rules. The imbedded program functions, f and g, are used to compose the rule for the structure involved. The process of composition is robust and independent of program size, but the intricacy of the function predicates is not so manageable. The tractability of the last step of this methodology (i.e., the proof of equivalence of two functions) will be largely determined by the user's skill in managing the compositions. The use of abstractions for program components is usually the key to control the amount of irrelevant detail being manipulated.

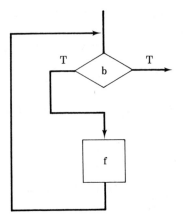

Figure 7-2.   The while. . do Structure.

The iterative program component, while..do, represented in flow-chart form (see Figure 7–2), has a program function:

$$[\text{while..do}] = \{ (X,Y) \mid (\exists k \geq 0)(\forall j, 0 \leq j < k)$$
$$b(f^j(X)) \wedge \neg b(f^k(X))$$
$$\wedge \ Y = f^k(X) \}$$

A termination requirement is built into this definition through the quantifier $\exists k \geq 0$.

These rules provide a sufficient set for composing program functions for arbitrary well-structured programs. Other less structured cases are treated in *Structured Programming: Theory and Practice* by R. C. Linger, H. D. Mills, and B. L. Witt (LMW79).

A direct comparison with the methodology of Chapter 5 can be seen by reconsidering the reversal problem on a data sequence. Using the stepwise process just delineated, the first step is the selection of a program, as shown below:

Reverse: Array A[1:N]

Integer I, N

Real T

for I: = 1 step 1 until ⌊n/2⌋

do [T: = A[I];

A[I]: = A[N − I + 1];

A[N − I + 1]: = T]

For this problem, the corresponding intended function may have been formulated as

$$\text{Reverse} = \{ (A,A') \mid A'[i] = A[\mid A \mid -i+1]\forall i \in 1..N\}$$

That is, the intended function acknowledges a very simple state vector, A, on which the transitions are defined. The program, on the other hand, is specified on an extended state vector, (I,N,T,A). Thus, one might immediately anticipate some logical difficulties in proving equivalence of the functions.

To continue the process, the derivation of the program function, [Reverse], proceeds from analysis of the program text. Thus, it is done in the same spirit as program tracing. But the analysis is symbolic rather than numeric. The program functions are obtained from the inside outward beginning with the [Exchange] segment:

$$[\text{Exchange}] = \{(I,N,T,A)(I,N,T',A')$$
$$\mid T' = A[I]$$
$$\wedge A'[N-I+1] = A[I]$$
$$\wedge A'[I] = A[N-I+1]\}$$

The body of the for..do structure is completed by the incrementing of I:

$$[\text{Exchange;inc}] = \{(I,N,T,A)(I',N,T'A')$$
$$\mid T' = A[I]$$
$$\wedge A'[N-I+1] = A[I]$$
$$\wedge A'[I] = A[N-I+1]$$
$$\wedge I' = I+1\}$$

The test part of the for..do is given as

$$[b] = I \leq \lfloor n/2 \rfloor$$

Thus, the for..do program function is

$$[\text{for..do}] = \{(I,N,T,A)(I',N,T',A')$$
$$\mid \exists k \geq 0 \ (\forall j, 1 \leq j < k)$$
$$[b]([\text{Exchange;inc}]^j(I,N,T,A))$$
$$\wedge \neg [b]([\text{Exchange;inc}]^k(I,N,T,A))$$
$$\wedge (I',N,T',A') = [\text{Exchange;inc}]^k(I,N,T,A)\}$$

The initialization parts of the program serve to collapse the domain of the program function by constraining I and N. Thus:

$$[\text{Reverse}] = \{(I,N,T,A),(I',N,T',A')$$
$$| \ \exists k \geq 0 \ (\forall j, \ 1 \leq j < k)$$
$$[b]([\text{Exchange;inc}]^i(I,N,T,A))$$
$$\Lambda \neg [b]([\text{Exchange;inc}]^k(I,N,T,A))$$
$$\Lambda (I',N,T',A') = [\text{Exchange;inc}]^k(I,N,T,A)$$
$$\Lambda \ I = 1$$
$$\Lambda \ N = |A| \ \}$$

Even a superficial comparison of the intended function, Reverse, with the program function, [Reserve], would suggest that proof of equivalence is not at hand. However, recognizing that the remaining steps deal only with mathematical structures (i.e., functions), the proof can be established by introducing surrogate functions and proving equivalence in small steps. For this problem, a workable strategy would be to convert each function to an equivalent recursive form. If termination can be separately argued (see Chapter 5), then the [for..do] program function has the form

$$[\text{for..do}] = \{(X,Y)|$$
$$[b] \ \Rightarrow \ Y = [\text{for..do}](f(X))$$
$$\Lambda \neg [b] \ \Rightarrow \ Y = X\}$$

The equivalence of this form to the original [for..do] can be established in general by inductive reasoning. Likewise, the intended function may be made recursive as in

$$\text{Reverse} = \{(N,A)(N',A')|$$
$$N = 0 \ \Rightarrow \ (A' = A)\Lambda(N' = 0)$$
$$\Lambda N > 0 \ \Rightarrow \ [A'[N] = A[|A| - N + 1]\Lambda A'[|A| - N + 1] = A[N]$$
$$\Lambda(N',A') = \text{Reverse}(N - 1,A)\}$$

Equivalence to the intended function is once again established by induction. Finally, the two recursive forms can be shown equivalent by induction. In summary, the proof of equivalence proceeds according to:

The intended function

↓

Recursive form of the intended function

‖

Recursive form of the program function

↑

Program function

↓

Termination

Particularly with loop-structured programs, the analysis is expected to rely on inductive reasoning to argue the equivalence of recursive functions. As abstractions are formulated and verified, it is often useful to substitute the intended (sub)-function for the derived (sub)-function. The validity of this substitution follows from the "Axiom of Replacement," which says that if P is a proper subprogram of Q, then

$$[P] = [P'] \Rightarrow [Q] = [Q']$$

where Q' is Q after P has been replaced by P'. The notion of "proper" here refers to having been built from well-structured building blocks (LMW79). This property allows whole loops, if. . then. . else's, etc., to be replaced by function labels once they are verified.

Example 7-1   Building a Test Suite for a Root-Finding Routine

Suppose a false position root-finding algorithm is to be tested for its ability to find the smallest root of a given function, f, in the domain (a,b) (see Figure 7-3).

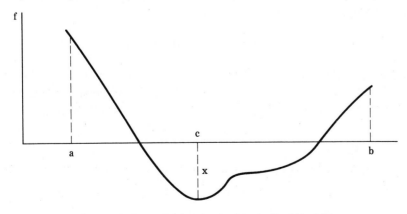

Figure 7-3. A Function of a Single Real Variable.

We can anticipate several pathologies in the algorithm based on the fact that it uses a false position technique:

1. It may converge to the root between c and b.
2. It may fail to converge to any root between a and b.

The obvious implementation would simply project the chord between the two current values of the function to the x-axis to obtain the abscissa of the next replacement abscissa (i.e., in Figure 7-4, x_3 would replace x_2).

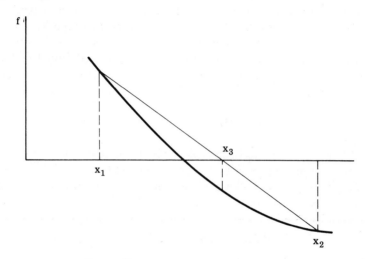

Figure 7–4.   A False Position Iteration.

For the purpose of this example, let us suppose that only one extremum, c, has been located in the function to be used in the tests. We may design a test such that

$$T = \{(x_1, x_2) \mid x_1 \text{ and } x_2 \,\epsilon(a,c)\}$$

where x_1 and x_2 are the starting values for the iteration. The test would be reliable since all cases succeed, but it would not be valid since the failure cases are systematically excluded. The criterion that gives

$$T = \{(a,c), (c,b)\}$$

would be unreliable since for the obvious implementation, one case succeeds and the other fails. The criterion defined by

$$T = \{(x_1, x_2) \mid x_1 \text{ and } x_2 \,\epsilon(c,b)\}$$

is both reliable and valid, but of course the obvious implementation would be found to fail in all cases.

But suppose a more sophisticated implementation was at hand, one that is designed to overcome the expected pathologies. The following criterion

$$T = \{(a,d), (e,b), (a,b) \mid d \le c \text{ and } e \ge c\}$$

would be valid, and if it is also reliable, then it can be concluded that the program is correct.

This example illustrates that the inference of correctness must often be made in the context of "expected pathologies." Adding this element to the development will often provide the needed process orientation to the theory.

Example 7-2   Testing Computations of Rational Functions

This example addresses some of the issues that arise from computations in which parts may be cancelled out by division. Suppose the intended function to be computed is

$$f(x) = \frac{(x - a_1)^2(x - a_2)}{(x - b_1)}$$

where a_1, a_2, and b_1 are distinct values, and the program was implemented as

$$p(x) = (x - a_2)$$

As a test, we might have chosen

$$T = \{x \mid (x - a)^2 = (x - b_1)\}$$

This test has two cases. It is reliable since it always succeeds, but it is not valid because the failure cases are systematically excluded. The case $x = a_2$ also succeeds since both functions evaluate to zero.

The test

$$T = \{x_1, x_2, x_3, x_4\}$$

where x_1, x_2, x_3, x_4 are distinct, is sufficient to distinguish the intended function, f, from p. If all the cases succeed (i.e., the test is reliable), then the program could not be p.

Even though the four distinct values are sufficient to distinguish f from p, it does not follow that p is correct. Assuming that the program actually was the given p, at least one of the four distinct cases would fail. Inferences of correctness are therefore denied.

REFERENCES

(BR75)   Brooks, F. P., *The Mythical Man-Month.* Reading. Mass.: Addison-Wesley Publishing Co., Inc., 1975.

(GG77)   Goodenough, J. B., and S. L. Gerhart, "Toward a Theory of Testing: Data Selection Criteria," *Current Trends in Programming Methodology,* vol. II Englewood Cliffs, N.J.: Prentice-Hall, Inc. 1977.

(Go79)   Goodenough, J. B., "A Survey of Program Testing Issues," *Research Directions in Software Technology.* Cambridge, Mass.: M.I.T. Press, 1979.

(LMW79)   Linger, R. C., H. D. Mills, and B. L. Witt, *Structured Programming: Theory and Practice.* Reading, Mass.: Addison-Wesley Publishing Co., Inc., 1979.

The Calculus
of Programs

Appendix A

The purpose of this section is to outline the theoretical foundations of the programming methodology that was discussed in Chapter 5. Much of this development appears in Dijkstra's *A Discipline of Programming* (Di76), which should serve as a valuable companion volume to this text in the study of software technology.

The calculus of programs begins with the definition of a weakest precondition written as WP(S,R):

> The weakest precondition with respect to a program, S, and a postcondition, R, is the set of all states that when subjected to the computation, S, will terminate and leave the state of computation in R.

Note that termination is a part of the definition. The calculus is established by "axiomatizing" the weakest precondition for a number of small building-block computations and defining some composition rules.

The axioms can best be visualized in terms of the semantics of small program designs; see items (a) through (d) below:

PROGRAM   SEMANTICS

(a) Assignment

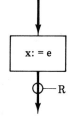

WP(x: = e,R) = R with
all occurrences of x
replaced by e.

(b) Sequences

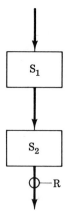

WP(S₁;S₂,R) =
WP(S₁,WP(S₂,R))

$$WP(S_1;S_2,R) = WP(S_1,WP(S_2,R))$$

PROGRAM   SEMANTICS

(c) If. . then. . else

WP(if B then S else S_2,R)
(B $\Rightarrow$ WP(S_1,R) and
$\urcorner$B $\Rightarrow$ WP(S_2,R))

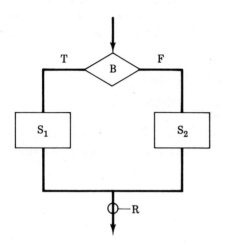

(d) While. . do

WP(While B do S,R) =
($\exists$k)((k $\geq$ 0) and H_k(R))
where
H_k(R) = (B$\wedge$WP(S,H_{k-1}(R)))
       or ($\urcorner$B$\wedge$R)
H_o(R) = $\urcorner$B$\wedge$R

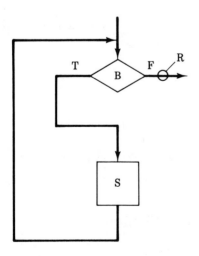

In the case of the while.. do, the intermediate function, $H_k(R)$, is the weakest precondition that the loop will terminate in k or fewer steps and leave the computation in a state defined by R.

As an aside, it should be noted that the structure of the while.. do axiom derives directly from the if.. then.. else axiom where the postconditions are not the same in each branch. That is, from the if.. then.. else, we have

$$H_k(R) = (B \Rightarrow WP(S,H_{k-1}(R)))\text{ and }\neg B \Rightarrow R)$$
$$H_o(R) = (\neg B \wedge R)$$

In addition to the axioms for the programming building blocks, there are some useful logical identities for the weakest preconditions; see items (a) through (e) below:

(a) No operation

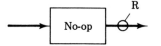 $WP(No\_op,R) = R$

(b) "Excluded miracle"

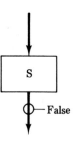 $WP(S,False) = False$

(c) Implication

$$(Q \Rightarrow R) \Rightarrow (WP(S,Q) \Rightarrow WP(S,R))$$

(d) Intersection

$$WP(S,Q) \wedge WP(S,R) = WP(S,Q \wedge R)$$

(e) Union for a deterministic program, S

$$WP(S,Q) \vee WP(S,R) = WP(S,Q \vee R)$$

These identities can be very useful when the weakest precondition is difficult or tedious to derive. In particular, the implication rule allows the choice of a stronger condition, Q, and the subsequent derivation with respect to Q with assurance that $WP(S,R)$ has not been violated.

The Syntax
of Ada Packages

Appendix B

The purpose of this appendix is to complete the syntactic details of Ada packages that were discussed in Section 4.5. At least a part of the richness of the concept derives from the variety of applications of packages and the variety of visibility options available for the internal components of packages.

Emphasizing the point that packages are separately compilable when they are declared as compilation units, the compilation unit is in the following form:

> compilation_unit:: =
>
> context_specification package_declaration
>
> | context_specification package_body
>
> | et al.

The context_specification names library units that are taken as relevant context to the package. If the compilation unit being defined is, in turn, part of the context of another unit, its name will be used in the context_specification:

> context_specification:: ={with_clause[use_clause]}
>
> with_clause:: = with unit_name{, unit_name}

The use_clause will be defined later. (*Note:* {   } indicates zero or more occurrences, and [   ] indicates optional occurrence.)

In addition to packages being "brought into" view by context_ specifications, they may appear as ordinary declarations as follows:

> declarative_part:: =
>
> {declaration | use_clause}
>
> {representation_specification}{package_declaration
>
> |package_body | package_body_stub | et al.}
>
> declaration:: = package_declaration
>
> | et al.

At this point, the package_declaration, the package_body, the package_body_stub, and the use_clause remain undefined. The representation_specification of the previous definition can be viewed as a separator only. The package_declaration may appear in three forms:

package_declaration:: = package_specification

| generic_package_declaration

| generic_package_instantiation

where for the last two options, we have

generic_package_declaration:: =

generic_part package_specification

generic_package_instantiation:: =

package identifier is generic_instantiation

The generic_part and generic_instantiation are beyond the scope of this discussion. The definition of package_specification remains to be defined in order to complete the definition of package_declaration. Thus:

package_specification:: =

package identifier is

{declarative_item}

[private

{declarative item}

{representation_specification}]

end[identifier];

Returning to the other options of declarative_part, we note the following:

use_clause:: = use package_name{, package_name};

The purpose of the use_clause is to allow importation of the contents of a package, thus making this context directly visible. There is an important exception, however, to the usual visibility rules in the case of imported package contents in that global declarations of the same thing will hid the one being imported.

The package_body is defined by

package_body:: =
    package body identifier is
        declarative_part
    [begin
        sequence_of_statements
    [exception
        {exception_handler}]]
    end[identifier];

package_body_stub:: =
    package body identifier is separate;

The package_body is the part of the package that is intended to be hidden. The purpose of the sequence_of_statements within the package_ body is to provide for initialization of items that may be declared within the package_body. These statements are executed upon elaboration of the package_body.

Verification of a Queue Management Package

Appendix C

The purpose of this discussion is to illustrate the role of program verification in the construction and coding of a queue management package. This development differs from Example 5.2 in that the objective is to obtain a more efficient algorithm, and the role of verification assertions in the final, coded product will be illustrated. In this version, the queue will be maintained as a "heap" which is viewed as a binary tree. The management of the heap will require that the priority of the entry associated with any node of the binary tree be greater than or equal to either of its descendents. (Ref: Aho, A. V., Hopcroft, J. E., and Ullman, J. D., The Design and Analysis of Computer Algorithms, Reading, Mass.: Addison-Wesley Publishing Co., 1974.)

In order to emphasize the point that this is a re-implementation of the program derived in Exercise 5.2, the visible part of the Ada package will be stated as before:

```
package QUEUE_MGR is
    type QUEUE_PAIR is record
    OBJECT: string (1 .. 20); —the object's name
    PRIORITY: integer;
    end record;
    procedure QUEUE_UP(P: in queue_pair);
    function UN_QUEUE return queue_pair;
end queue_mgr;
```

Thus, the problem remains one of designing the implementation of the QUEUE_MGR package. It is convenient to represent the queue as a linear array of queue_pair's, i.e.

queue:array(1 .. max_size) of queue_pair

where

$1 < \, = \text{next\_space} < \, = \text{max\_size} + 1$

(Note: Since Ada commentary is to be generated, the assertions will be expressed in the Ada character set.)

The heap structure will be created by computing indices on the queue according to: if the index of the parent is j, then the first child (if it exists) is at 2*j and the second child (if it exists) is at 2*j + 1.

Gathering the preceding observations together, we can now assert some universal pre- and postconditions on the use of the queue manager:

(next_space> = 1) and
(next_space< = max_size + 1) and
is_heap

where is_heap is

[for all j in 1 .. (next_space − 1)/2]H[j]

and H[j] is

(queue(j).priority> = queue(2*j).priority) and
[(2*j + 1 > next_space − 1) or queue(j).priority> = queue(2*j + 1).
priority]

That is, upon entering and leaving the queue manager, the next_space must be within bounds, and the queue must be a heap.

An important property of the heap follows directly from the assertions. Stated as a theorem, it can be shown that:

Theorem: Upon entering the queue manager, the highest priority queue_pair in the queue is in the first position of the queue, i.e., queue(1).priority> = queue(j).priority for all j in 2 .. next_space − 1.

The proof of this follows from the transitivity of the "> = " relation and the observation that 2*j and 2*j + 1 indexing for the nodes of the heap will cover the entire domain 2.. next_space − 1. The above theorem leads to the statement of the additional postcondition for the un_queue operation as

(ret_val = queue'(1)) and
(next_space = next_space' − 1)

where the preconditions are extended to include

(queue = queue') and
(next_space = next_space')

For the queue_up operation, the postconditions are extended to include

(p in queue) and
next_space = next_space' + 1)

The partially constructed package body thus appears as:

```
package body QUEUE_MGR is
    QUEUE_EMPTY,QUEUE_FULL:exception;
    MAX_SIZE: integer: = 256;  —arbitrary max_size
    NEXT_SPACE: integer: = 1;
    QUEUE: array(1 .. max_size) of queue_pair;
    procedure QUEUE_UP(P: in queue_pair) is
    begin
        if next_space > max_size then
            raise queue_full;
        end if;
    —— (next_space > = 1) and
    —— (next_space < = max_size) and
    —— is_heap and
    —— (queue = queue') and
    —— (next_space = next_space')
    —— queue(next_space): = p;
    —— next_space: = next_space + 1;
    ——
    ——
    —— restore the heap
    ——
    ——
    —— (next_space > = 1) and
    —— (next_space < = max_size + 1) and
    —— is_heap and
    —— (next_space = next_space' + 1) and
    —— (p is in the queue)
    exception
        when queue_full = > put("The queue is full.");
    end queue_up;
    function UN_QUEUE return queue_pair is
        RET_VAL: queue_pair;
```

```
      begin
           if next_space = 1 then
                raise queue_empty;
           end if;
--  (next_space > = 1) and
--  (next_space < = max_size) and
--  is_heap and
--  (queue = queue') and
--  (next_space = next_space')
                ret_val: = queue(1);
                next_space: = next_space - 1;
                queue(1): = queue(next_space);

--

--

--  restore the heap

--

--

--  (next_space > = 1) and
--  (next_space < = max_size) and
--  is_heap and
--  (ret_val = queue'(1)) and
--  (next_space = next_space' - 1)
           exception
                when queue_empty = > put("The queue is empty.");
           end un_queue;
      begin
           console: = null; --for text_io
      end queue_mgr;
```

At this stage of the construction, the verification assertions have been added as commentary to the package components. (Note: The "__" indicates that the remainder of the line is commentary.) The return value (i.e. ret_val) has been created in the case of un_queue, and the parameter, p, has been placed on the queue in the case of queue_up.

In both cases the queue is no longer a heap. Thus, the segments denoted by "restore the heap" are yet to be designed.

In the case of an un_queue operation, the heap is restored by "sifting" the out-of-place item upward in the tree. In the case of the queue _up operation, the queue(next_space − 1) item is out of place and must be sifted downward. The sifting operation is to be realized as a loop. Whether sifting upward or downward, there will be at most one node in the tree which does not have the property, H[j]. A universal loop invariant is immediately established to capture the condition: The H[j] property must be maintained in all but one place, i.e.

$$Q[k] = [\text{for all } j \text{ in } 1 .. (\text{next\_space} - 1)/2, j/ = k] \, H[j].$$

In contrast to methodology illustrated in Chapter 5, at this point we have a loop invariant without the relaxation of the postcondition. However, the postcondition can be established by noting that

$$Q[k] \text{ and } H[k] = \text{is\_heap}$$

Since H[k] is not defined beyond the limits of the queue, the above expression must be refined to

$$Q[k] \text{ and } [\, H[k] \text{ or } (k \text{ not in } 1 .. (\text{next\_space} - 1)/2)]$$

which is of the form, Q and not B, thus

$$B = \text{not } H[k] \text{ and } [k \text{ in } 1 .. (\text{next\_space} - 1)/2]$$

which, in turn, establishes a universal loop termination test.

It is interesting to observe at this point that, although two loops, sift-up and sift-down, are being designed, they are being verified together. A "universal loop invariant" and a "universal loop test" have emerged. A common "restore heap" program structure can be visualized as

```
initialize k
while B
  loop
  exchange parent and child nodes
  update k
  end loop
```

The "exchange parent and child nodes" component is required to establish the truth of H[k]. This program segment would appear as:

```
-- exchange parent and child nodes
-- Q[k] and B
if (queue(2*k).priority > = queue(2*k + 1).priority) or
    2*k + 1 > next_space - 1 then
    t: = queue(k);
    queue(k): = queue(2*k);
    queue(2*k); = t;
else
    t: = queue(k);
    queue(k): = queue(2*k + 1);
    queue(2*k + 1): = t;
end if;
-- H[k]
```

The verification of this component follows from viewing it as:

```
if test_siblings[k] then s1;
                else s2;
end if;
```

where test_siblings[k] is

$$queue(2*k).priority > = queue(2*k + 1).priority$$
$$or \; 2*k + 1 > next\_space - 1$$

It can be proven that

$$Q[k] \text{ and } B \text{ and } test\_siblings[k] = \; > wp(s1, H[k])$$

and

$$Q[k] \text{ and } B \text{ and not } test\_siblings[k] = \; > wp(s2, H[k])$$

The additional generated commentary is shown for the two branches of the exchange.

-- exchange parent and child nodes
-- Q[k] and B
if (queue(2*k).priority > = queue(2*k + 1).priority) or
    2*k + 1 > next_space – 1 then
        –– queue(2*k).priority > = queue(k).priority and
        –– (2*k + 1 > next_space – 1 or
        –– queue(2*k).priority > = queue(2*k + 1).priority)
    t: = queue(k);
    queue(k): = queue(2*k);
    queue(2*k): = t;
    else
        –– queue(2*k + 1).priority > = queue(2*k).priority and
        –– (2*k + 1 > next_space – 1 or
        –– queue(2*k + 1).priority > = queue(k).priority)
    t: = queue(k);
    queue(k): = queue(2*k + 1);
    queue(2*k + 1): = t;
end if;
--H[k]

Although the remaining verification steps can be pursued in a universal form by creating a variable denoting whether the operation is a sift-up or a sift-down operation, dividing the verification at this point facilitates the remaining reasoning processes. Thus, the universal loop invariant will be augmented by those conditions which are specific to the operation being performed, i.e.

Q[k] and sift-up[k]

for sift-up, and

Q[k] and sift-down[k]

for sift-down, where

sift-up[k] = queue(k/2).priority > = queue(2*k).priority
            and queue(k/2).priority > = queue(2*k + 1).priority

and

sift-down[k] = (for i in 0 .. 3)queue(k).priority> = queue(4*k + i).
priority
and [queue(k).priority> = queue(2*k).priority
or queue(k).priority> = queue(2*k + 1).priority]

There will be four internal proofs to be completed, namely:

not H[k] and Q[k] and sift-up[k] and test_siblings[k] = >
wp(SLU, Q[k] and sift-up[k])
not H[k] and Q[k] and sift-up[k] and not test_siblings[k] = >
wp(SRU,Q[k] and sift-up[k])
not H[k] and Q[k] and sift-down[k] and test_siblings[k] = >
wp(SLD,Q[k] and sift-down[k])
Not H[k] and Q[k] and sift-down[k] and not test_siblings[k] = >
wp(SLU,Q[k] and sift-down[k])

where

SLU is sl;k: = 2*k;
SRU is s2;k: = 2*k + 1;
SLD is s1;k: = k/2;
SRD is s2;k: = k/2;

(Note: s1 and s2 are branches of the conditional defined above.) All four
of these proofs follow a pattern as illustrated below for the SLU case:

wp(SLU,Q[k] and sift-up[k]) =
wp(s1,H[k] and H[2*k + 1] and queue(k).priority> = queue(4*k).
priority and queue(k).priority> = queue(4*k + 1).
priority)=
queue(2*k).priority> = queue(2*k).priority and
queue(2*k).priority> = queue(2*k + 1).priority and
queue(2*k).priority> = queue(4*k).priority and
queue(2*k).priority> = queue(4*k + 1).priority

Taking these factors in succession, it is noted that

not H[k] and test_siblings[k] = > queue(2*k).priority> = queue (2*k).priority

test_siblings[k] = > queue(2*k).priority> = queue(2*k + 1). priority

Q[k] = > H[2*k] = > queue(2*k).priority> = queue(4*k).priority and   queue(2*k).priority> = queue(4*k + 1). priority

Finally, it must be shown that the extended loop invariants are true upon entering the loop. The sift-up[1] and sift-down[(next_space − 1)/2] will be assumed true since they refer to conditions beyond the tree. It suffices to observe that any replacement of queue(1) does not change the validity of Q[1], i.e.

wp(queue(1): = anything, Q[k]) = Q[1]

Likewise

wp(next_space: = next_space − 1, Q[1]) = (for all i in 1 .. next_space − 2) H[i]

Which is clearly implied by is_heap at the same point.
    For the purpose of termination, it is observed that

(next_space − 1 − k)* integer(not H[k] or k > (next_space − 1)/2)

is a well founded set for sifting upward, and

(k − 1)*integer(not H[k])

is a well founded set for sifting downward.
    What follows is the full Ada package together with the derived commentary. The reasoning process used here led to a great deal of commonality in the Ada text between the queue_up and the un_queue operations. Thus, the verification effort 'was not nearly as great as might be suggested by the program text. This version was compiled on the STC-Ada (B1.0 release) compiler designed by the Western Digital Corporation. Although the verification left very few gaps in the confidence that the program was a faithful representation of the intended package, testing has confirmed in a limited way that the package is workable.

```
with stc_io;
use stc_io;
package QUEUE_MGR is
    type QUEUE_PAIR is record
        OBJECT: string(1 .. 20); —the object's name
        PRIORITY: integer;
    end record;
    procedure QUEUE_UP(P: in queue_pair);
    function UN_QUEUE return queue_pair;
end queue_mgr;


——

——

——

——


package body QUEUE_MGR is
    ——is_heap = [for all j in 1 .. (next_space − 1)/2] H[j]
    ——Q[k] = [for all j in 1 .. (next_space − 1)/2,j/ = k] H[j].
    ——test_siblings[k] = queue(2*k).priority > = queue(2*k + 1).
    ——      priority or 2*k + 1 > next_space − 1
    QUEUE_EMPTY,QUEUE_FULL:exception;
    MAX_SIZE: integer: = 256: —arbitrary max_size
    NEXT_SPACE: integer: = 1;
    T: queue_pair;
    QUEUE: array(1 .. max_size) of queue_pair;
    function H(K:in integer) return boolean is
        begin
        return (queue(k).priority > = queue(2*k).priority)
            and (2*k + 1 > next_space − 1 or else
            queue(k).priority > = queue(2*k + 1).priority;
    end h;
    procedure QUEUE_UP(P:in queue_pair) is
    K:integer;
    begin
        if next_space > max_size then
            raise queue_full;
```

```
        end if;
--  (next_space > = 1) and
--  (next_space < = max_size) and
--  is_heap and
--  (queue = queue') and
--  (next_space = next_space')
        queue(next_space): = p;
        next_space: = next_space + 1;

--

--

--  restore the heap
k: = (next_space − 1)/2;
while k > = 1 and then (not h(k))
loop  -- Q[k]
        --  and (for all i in 0 .. 3)[queue(k).priority > =
        --        queue(4*k + i).priority
        --        or 4*k + i > next_space − 1]
        -- and [queue(k).priority > = queue(2*k).priority
        --        or queue(k).priority > = queue(2*k).priority
        --        or 2*k + 1 > next_space − 1]
        -- exchange parent and child nodes
        if 2*k + 1 > next_space − 1 or else
            (queue(2*k).priority > = queue(2*k + 1).priority) then
                -- not H[k] and Q[k] and sift_down[k] and test_
                    siblings[k]
                t: = queue(k);
                queue(k): = queue(2*k);
                queue(2*k): = t;
                else
                -- not H[k] and Q[k] and sift_down[k] and test_
                    siblings[k]
                t: = queue(k);
                queue(k): = queue(2*k + 1);
                queue(2*k + 1): = t;
            end if;
```

```
    ——H[k]
    k: = k/2;
    end loop;
——

——

——(next_space > = 1) and
——(next_space < = max_size + 1) and
——is_heap and
——(next_space = next_space' + 1) and
——(p is in the queue)
exception
    when queue_full = > put("The queue is full.");
end queue_up;
function UN_QUEUE return queue_pair is
    RET_VAL:queue_pair;
    K:integer;
    begin
        if next_space = 1 then
            raise queue_empty;
        end if;
——(next_space > = 1) and
——(next_space < = max_size) and
——is_heap and
——(queue = queue') and
——(next_space = next_space')
        ret_val: = queue(1);
        next_space: = next_space — 1;
        queue(1): = queue(next space);
        ——

        ——

        ——restore the heap
k: = 1;
while k < = (next_space — 1)/2 and then (not h(k))
    loop ——Q[k]
```

```
        -- and queue(k/2). priority > = queue(2*k).priority
        -- and [queue(k/2).priority > = queue(2*k + 1).priority
        --    or 2*k + 1 > next_space - 1]
    --exchange parent and child nodes
 if 2*k + 1 > next_space - 1 or else
    (queue(2*k).priority > = queue(2*k + 1).priority) then
        -- not H[k] and Q[k] and sift_up[k] and test_siblings[k]
        t: = queue(k);
        queue(k): = queue(2*k);
        queue(2*k): = t;
        k: = 2*k;
        else
        -- not H[k] and Q[k] and sift_up[k] and test_siblings[k]
        t: = queue(k);
        queue(k): = queue(2*k + 1);
        queue(2*k + 1): = t;
        k: = 2*k + 1;
    end if;
    --H[k]
    end loop;

    --
--(next_space > = 1) and
--(next_space > = max_size) and
--is_heap and
--(ret_val = queue'(1)) and
--(next_space = next_space' - 1)
    return ret_val;
    exception
        when queue_empty = > put("The queue is empty.");
    end un_queue;
end queue_mgr;
```

Index